Seoul

Food

Short stories of a Korean American
Living in Los Angeles

Sarai Koo

SPICES Publications
13337 South Street, Ste. 770
Cerritos, CA 90703

Copyright © 2014 Sarai Koo

Disclaimer: This publication contains the opinions and concepts of its author. The book is based on real life stories of second generation Korean Americans. To protect people's identities, the character names and minor details have been changed.

Cover Design: Helen Ho

ISBN - 10: 0990775003
ISBN-13: 978-0-9907750-0-3

DEDICATION

To everyone. Let us unite, bridge differences, and value others as ourselves.

CONTENTS

PART 1. POJAGI

PART 2. BIBIMBAP AND BANCHAN

PART 3. JEON

PART 1

POJAGI

Pojagi is variously-shaped multicolored squares of linen that seamlessly and other times awkwardly stitch together to form a larger piece of material.

Pojagi

"*Halmoni*! *Hajima*!" All of us—mom, dad, sister, brother, and me—yelled at grandma to stop ruining the objects in our home. My dad's mom rampaged through our house with a pair of silver shears, grabbing and cutting pieces of our clothing, big blankets, and other seemingly useless patches of fabric. Then, during odd hours of the night, she took those pieces of old and new fabric to make oddly-patched small pillow covers out of them without our permission. Despite our telling her to stop, her stingy and argumentative tendencies prevented her from listening to us. Whenever she came over during her unannounced visits, we became stressed and made up reasons to get livid with one another for the littlest issues. *Halmoni* had a way of destroying whole objects into fragmented pieces to create her version of a whole pillow. Her way was the right way, and when all of us didn't listen to her, she created a chaos that quenched our spirits.

Weh-halmoni, my mom's mom, was different. As a former school principal and master calligraphist, she was full of wisdom and grace, a living example of a phenomenal Korean female with etiquette and manners. She would sit for hours with her calligraphy brush and inkstone, perfectly inscribing ancient characters, stark black-and-white poetry that spoke of longevity, blessing, and creativity. Her peaceful and elegant spirit as a great orator and leader was evident in the way she spoke, wrote, and lived, despite her gender and the other oppressions she had faced during the Korean War. When *Weh-halmoni* came to visit us every so often before she passed away in Korea, she showed how to mend broken hearts and appreciate differences by never getting upset at a person or situation. Her love transcended to everyone wherever she went.

Weh-halmoni was one of the few people who helped me recognize that my identity and the multiple cities I would come to live in could combine to make peace with others and myself. However, the process of weaving the odd-shaped pieces of my life into one whole took time.

My siblings and I were born in America and grew up in different parts of Los Angeles. LA reminded me of *pojagi,* diverse people living in a condensed community with segregated ethnic lines, or living in the seamlessly blended boundaries where our backgrounds converged. And my friends–whose skin color ranged from fair skinned to rich brown, socioeconomic statuses from poor to rich, height from short to tall, and weight from thin to overweight–were like the United Nations. We looked different on the outside, but in my view, we were one. We were all human beings.

However, I soon came to realize that my parents–and the world at large–did not so firmly agree with my idealistic "we are all human beings" perspective. My parents distinctly emphasized our Korean identity. They spoke to us in Korean and told us we were Korean.

"Nuh-neun han-gook sah-ram-e-ya weh-nyah-ha-myun appa rang Umma ga han-gook sa-ram e-ni-ggah. Gue-ruh-ni-ggan, nu-neun han-gook mal-eul ar-ah-yah ha-go eeh-jeu-myun an-dwe." You are a Korean person because your dad and mom are Korean. Therefore, you need to know the Korean language and not forget it.

Similar to many second-generation Koreans who might forget how to write and speak Korean in such a patchwork city, my siblings and I were forced to attend Korean school to reinforce our Korean-ness. I really didn't like it. The teachers would speak in Korean and punish little Korean-looking children like myself when we spoke in English. Memories of being punished more than actually learning Korean flooded my mind. At the numerous Korean schools my siblings and I attended, my punishment consisted of writing the Korean alphabet 50 times or sitting in the corner of the room with arms raised high above my head. This just made my shoulders hurt and nurtured in me disdain for learning the Korean language.

As little children, we listened to our parents and would complacently respond in Korean, "Yes, we are Korean." However, as we grew older and began attending public elementary school, our allegiance to being identified as Koreans shifted. Our identities were being redefined in the school system where the American way was perceived as the better way. When my parents lectured us about our Korean heritage and pride, I got flashbacks of my teachers telling me, "You live in America, so you need to speak in English." These words would seep into my brain: Speak English. Be American.

I didn't know whom to believe. My teachers were the ones who were educating me so that I could be a fully-certifiable, assimilated, accent-free American citizen. But my parents were my parents. As soon as I got home from school, having been filled up with English words and faces, I felt as though I were stepping across an invisible border into an imagined Korea–a Korea that my parents had taught me, carefully built and preserved from their own childhood memories. Everyday I shuttled to and from these two countries, trying to navigate *me*.

My siblings and I eventually chose to exchange our Korean identity for being more American. Rejecting my Korean-ness, I told myself that I was an American; I would lose the accent, adopt the mainstream culture, and be more like my "other" friends.

"Speak English. We live in America!" My sister and I often said to Mom when we didn't understand the complex Korean words she used. We thought we were right because that's what students and teachers told us.

"*Nuh-neun han-gook sah-ram-e-ya!*" You're Korean! My parents scolded us right back. We rolled our eyes. They didn't know. We were Americans because we were born in America. After such outbursts, my siblings and I received *mae maes*, physical and verbal beatings.

In public, mom would speak loudly to me in Korean. Once, I heard an older white lady with orangey-brownish hair who peered at us from the corner of her eyes, whispering, "These Orientals need to learn how to speak English. We're in America."

So, I spoke back to Mom in English.

"*Moh?*" What? She responded, even louder. "*Hanguk mal heh.*" Speak in Korean. She didn't understand me. I think the only English she knew was *No, McDonalds, haembeogeo,* and *me no Engrish.*

"*Hanguk mal heh,*" my mom repeated.

At this, Orange-Brown-Haired Lady, who had continued to peer at us, came up, pointed a finger at my mom's chest, and said,

"You're in America. You should learn to speak in English."

Orange-Brown-Haired Lady was not the first person, nor the last, to say these kinds of things. During those times, I would only feel shame that my parents did not speak English, shame that they were not American, and shame that this merited glaring stares and whispers from strangers. We were seen as foreigners, recent immigrants, or, simply, Chinese people.

"Are you Chinese?" A chubby boy with tight curls and scrutinizing hazel eyes inquired. My siblings and I were cornered against the schoolyard fence during recess.

"No," we replied.

"Are you Japanese?"

"No."

They went through a laundry list of nationalities.

"I'm an American," my sister, Janice, finally declared.

"No, you're not," another student retorted.

"We were born in America, so we're Americans," I stated.

"No, you're not," a different student remarked.

"I'm Korean," my brother, Frank, said. I glared at him.

"Okay," the two students agreed.

Another student chimed in, "Then how come you're here in America when you're Korean? Shouldn't you live in your country?"

I didn't know how to respond. Did they ask African Americans to go back to Africa? Or Caucasians to go back to the Caucasus mountains? It was puzzling, and I wondered how to determine if a person were American or not.

At first, I thought it was the color of one's skin. But being in LA, skin color was not a good indicator. We came in many shades. I then thought, perhaps it was one's accent.

"Where is your accent from?" John asked me. He had sandy brown hair and light skin.

"What accent?" I asked.

"That. That accent," he stated again.

"What accent?" I remarked.

"Stop joking around. You have this accent. Where are you from?"

I stared at him, thinking, *uh, he knows I'm from America.* "I'm from America. I was born and raised in America."

"No, I mean, where are you from?" He wasn't satisfied.

"I'm from America. I was born and raised in the States." I thought if I said "States," that would make it clearer.

"Fine, where were your parents born?"

". . . Korea." Once again, I felt somewhere in the middle . . . and nowhere.

Like my parents, my school friends couldn't see that we were like *pojagi*, different pieces that harmoniously created one whole human society.

"How much can you see? Do you see me?" the curly, orange-haired, freckled-face James asked me one day. Uneven brown spots formed a curtain behind which his fair white skin peeked through.

"I can see you. Why?" I insisted, while laughing. I wore glasses, so, of course, I could see him. I furrowed my forehead to open my eyes wider and show him that I could see him. Around us, some of my friends stared, listening and silent.

"Your eyes are really small. I didn't want to mention it, but I always wondered if you were able to see."

He put his fingers next to his eyes and slanted them to show me how my eyes looked according to him. I froze, staring blankly at him. My friends laughed at what James was doing.

"Yeah! That's right. His eyes looks like yours now," a classmate shouted.

"Hahahaha! That's so funny."

"Ching Chong," said another.

Other people laughed, and so I chuckled as well.

"That's so stupid," I remarked. "My eyes aren't slanted. My eyes are like yours." What an idiotic question. My eyes were big. My mom told me they were.

After James's slant eyes, I went to the restroom and stared at myself in the mirror. Analyzing my face, I couldn't figure out why people thought my eyes were slanted. They were as big as James's. Slanted eyes? No. Mom would confirm that my eyes weren't slanted.

"Mom, someone from school asked me if I could see because he said my eyes were small and slanted," I informed her. Mom had big, round eyes that covered almost one-third of her face.

"No, your eyes are actually big," she responded. "Other Asians want your eyes because they are big. *Chan gan ha ji ma.*" Don't worry about it.

Listening to my mother's advice, I went back to school as my American self. When I saw my peers, instead of seeing the differences as divisive, I saw them as a way to potentially create a new and unique pojagi, just like *Weh-Halmoni* did at home. With that in mind, even if we didn't look alike, I hoped that our English language could be a thread that sewed us together.

"I'ma gonna get to somin to ead. Do you come wanna?" I asked one of my friends during lunch.

"What did you say?" She replied. "I don't know what you are trying to say. Can you repeat yourself?"

I said it again. "I'ma gonna get to somin to ead. You come wanna?"

"I don't understand what you're saying on top of your accent. But, I think you're asking if I want to have lunch with you. Sure!"

The challenge of unified diversity continued in middle school, where we had a diverse body of students but very little thread to connect us. On random days, people who I didn't know would walk by and say, "Ching Chong." On several occasions, they would slant their eyes and ask me to do some karate moves. I suppose they didn't know that they were speaking nonsensical words and that Karate is actually a Japanese martial art; Tae Kwon Do is Korean. After a while, I just ignored them.

When I went to high school, I experienced for the first time the strangeness of a homogeneous community, where our differences were stifled. My family had decided to move to a predominantly Asian neighborhood. At my new school, the teachers, administrators, and non-Asians had a high esteem for Asians. They thought we were very smart. A rumor went around that Asians had a genetic mutation that made us born geniuses. It was also believed that Asians who were in regular classes or got into trouble struggled because their classes were not challenging enough. One Asian student who was suspended for getting into a fight was later transferred to a magnet school because he was deemed too smart for his old environment, which was not conducive for his intelligence and growth.

When I went to college, I thought the professors would be less naïve and open to differences. I was wrong.

"Where are you from?" Professor Hanna inquired. She was a white professor whose concentration was in identity and cultural studies.

"Huh? Me?" I asked. She tilted her head downward and peered into my eyes as if I didn't hear her.

"America?" I said doubtfully.

"No, I mean, where are you from?" She asked me again.

"You mean where I am from?" I paused and wondered what her point was. "America. I was born in America." I replied. I didn't ask why she was questioning me. Because of her area of emphasis, I thought she must have a scholarly reason.

"I mean, what is your nationality?" she asked again.

"Korean?" Now I wasn't sure if she was asking me a trick question.

"Well, I'm only asking you because you write like a student who came from a different country."

For the past 10 weeks, I had been writing and speaking to her in English. I wondered why this expert connected my outer exterior with my writing ability, or felt she had the right to tell me where I was from, and then state I wrote like a foreigner. Was my written language not in English? Did I have an accent? These unanswered questions were still roaming in my mind. Wherever I went, my identity was questioned. Though my outer appearance could not be changed to a fair-skinned Western woman, I worked on my diction and pronunciation to reduce my Korean accent.

"Wow, you speak English good!" An older white lady said while I was asking a store clerk where I could find detergent.

I smiled and replied, "Yes, I speak English well."

"When did you come to America? Because your accent is really good," She remarked inquisitively.

"I was born here."

"Oh my, really. I could have sworn you came from a different country," her eyes opened a little wider. "Well," she continued, "I remember when the war happened. You Orientals came over to America. It was sad to see a lot of you get moved. By the way, I love Chinese food."

I chuckled and smiled.

"I believe the 'move' you are referring to is the Japanese internment camp. Is this what you mean?"

"Why, yes! That's right. It was so sad for the United States to make a mistake."

Grinning, I stated, "Don't we all?"

"I'm just glad we're becoming more international," she continued. "I wouldn't know what to do without Chinese food. I just had some last night."

"I'm actually Korean. I do like Chinese food, but Korean food is different." Despite her international outlook, she was like *Halmoni* who created her version of unity. We Asians were meshed into one category.

Her eyes raised. "I see," she said.

I nodded my head, trying to leave the conversation and get to another part of the store.

"Well," she smiled. "You sure sound like an American, but you sure don't look like one."

Navigating through two countries and a *pojagi* county like Los Angeles, and then constantly being asked where I was from, brought me to visit the motherland in my early twenties.

"Excuse me," said a Korean lady on the street in Seoul. "I like how you curled your hair. How did you do it?" From my partial knowledge of Korean, I pieced together what she said.

"Um, *nah* (I) *son* (hand) *moe-li* (hair) uh," I tried putting the Korean sentence together.

Seeing me struggle to string together a sentence in her native tongue, she quickly said, "I'm sorry. I thought you were Korean."

"*Na-neun han-gook sa-lam ya,*" I tried reassuring her that I was a Korean person. "*Han-guk sa-lam chuh-rum boi-ji-man, . . .* (You look like a Korean, but . . .)," she whispered to herself and started walking away. She glanced once more at me, shook her head, and went her way, dismissing my curled locks and me. I felt like I had in Korean school as a little girl—punished for not being able to speak Korean properly.

Great. When I was in America, I wasn't a *real* American because I didn't look like it, even though I am a U.S. citizen. When I was in Korea, even though I look Korean, I wasn't *really* a Korean because I couldn't speak Korean fluently. I had arrived in Seoul thinking I had come home to my roots, only to realize I was perceived as a foreigner.

With each negative experience I encountered, layers of pain patched my soul and sometimes punctured my heart. As a child, my limited view led me to believe I was the only one like this, but hearing people and seeing constant divisions between "us" versus "them," and "the have" versus "the have not's," this pain that was once all mine was actually endemic. We all had our hearts wounded by someone from our past. We tried covering our pain or pretended we didn't have any, but when we pointed out a fault or said a negative comment to another person just because he or she looked different, the wounds became evident.

My two *halmonis* helped me understand this pain. Both of them took pieces to create a whole masterpiece; yet, the approaches they used led to two different outcomes. *Halmoni,* dad's mom, created a pillow using different irregular and regular material throughout our house without our permission. She said and did what she wanted and had no problem using negative words to demean us. Her damaging character traits grated us, and our family members often fought, sometimes for no apparent reason. Hearing, learning, and understanding each other could have resolved our issues, but when one person pierced the soul of another, the pain surfaced until every one in the household was hurt. Our lives were like a broken cycle that could not be mended. *Halmoni* reminded me of the way many people interacted with others.

Weh-halmoni, however, had the best solution to bridge differences. *Pojagi* is also wrapping cloth that holds and covers the important things. *Weh-halmoni* wrapped people's painful differences with love. Though she may have been oppressed for being a Korean female leader during her era, she understood that the only way to stop the contention was to interweave regular and irregular people into one beautiful and harmonious masterpiece. Love was transcendent, and when I thought about her *pojagi,* the cloth represented not only a covering but also a precious present. My hope was for people from diverse ethnic groups, cultures, and backgrounds to interweave pieces of their irregular and regular shaped selves together to mend our hurt and pierced souls. If *Weh-halmoni* could do it, so could I and others.

17

My *Gah-Jok*, My Family

"How can anyone live in America with $200!?" I exclaimed. My dad came into my room to shut my blinds and share his random conversations with me.

"When you are a recent immigrant, that's the only amount you can bring with you," my dad explained. He shared about his expedition from Korea to the land of opportunity.

"We were only allowed to bring this amount."

"Is this why many immigrants suffer when they come to the United States? Why did you want to come to America?"

"I came to America in search of a better life." He shared how his life in the 70s was parallel with the other Korean immigrants. South Korea was still struggling from the aftermath of the Korean War. He, like the rest of the immigrants, heard about the wonderful life a person could attain only in America. He bought into the ideology that *anything was possible in America.*

So he flew into Los Angeles with $200 and worked in the junkyard as his first job. The land of opportunity was definitely endless when people's trash became another person's treasure. My dad, who saved and used someone else's trash as our homely furnishings, truly represented the opportunity to live well no matter how little money we had.

"So, does this mean I'm a junk baby?" I asked him. I imagined my dad in oily overalls scrounging through piles of reeking, rotting trash and bringing home our next antiquated goods. Was that where he got our crib and kitchen table?

"No, silly. You are not. That was my first job and you weren't born yet," he assured me. "We now have enough money to buy things. The junk we have are items we don't use at home and throw away."

"What do I tell people when they ask about me and my family?"

"Tell them you are Sarai!" he laughed at me. "You see? You *Seh-La.* You *Seh* like a bird and *La* sing like a bird. You fly high and sing and shout for a better life! You know? *Seh-La.*" He was motioning his arms as if he were flying and singing off-key.

19

I stared at him, trying to hold back my laughter.

My name is Sarai and I'm Korean. My name was misspelled when I was born at a hospital in Los Angeles. When my mom was pregnant, she became a born-again believer, and the pastor at her church helped to spell my name.

"How do you spell Sarah? *Seh-La* sounds like a beautiful name for a Korean baby living in America," my mom asked her pastor in Korean.

"Oh, let us see...eh," he paused for a moment, using the oft-uttered *"eh"* that Koreans interject when an English word doesn't come easily. It wasn't *uhm, like,* or *you know.* It was *eh.*

"Eh, S-A-R-A-I." The pastor came to America before my parents, so my mom trusted his advice.

Born and raised in Los Angeles, I grew up being made fun of because of the spelling of my name. Classmates would mock me for having a name and a look that was different from theirs, from their world.

"Did your parents not know how to spell your name?"

"No," I often responded.

Teachers, who I'd thought knew how to read, often called me by weird names. "Is Sorry here?"

Classmates laughed.

"I'm not sure if this is right. Safari? Suh-ree?"

"No, it's Sara with an I!"

Rather than getting embittered by their remarks, I learned to use my name to crack jokes with them.

"HAHAHA! My parents messed up! It's so funny that they would write it as S-A-R-A-I. They thought my name was supposed to be spelled with an '*i*' instead of '*h.*' Either way, my name is unique. Isn't it unique for a Korean female?"

Growing up, when people asked for the spelling of my name, they paused, slightly moved their heads in the opposite direction, and inquired, "Isn't it supposed to be Sarah with an *h?*"

"Depends," I grinned with glee. "I don't know. My parents messed up my name."

"I see."

It was not until later in life when I began to read the Bible that I realized I was a beautiful princess, mother of all people. Sarai was Abraham's wife, a most beautiful woman who couldn't get pregnant until she was past her child-bearing days. The next time people asked me where my name came from, I joyfully shared with them who I was.

"I am a princess who is the mother of all," I sometimes stated.

People stoically stared at me and tilted their heads to the side. To avoid confusing them, I continued, "My name is in the Bible. I thought my parents messed my name up, but now I know they must have been geniuses for giving me a unique name." Their heads tilted in the opposite direction. Whether people thought I was crazy, I smiled and sometimes waved my hands as if I were a princess on the Rose Parade. My responses were often unpredictable.

Other than myself, my parents gave birth to my older sister Janice and younger brother named Frank. My parents wanted my older sister to be nice. "You nice, ok? Remember your name," my parents often said to my sister. My sister, whether she was nice or not, was stuck with her name.

My brother? I don't know why my parents named him Frank. Maybe my mom liked Frank Sinatra's music.

Growing up, Frank lacked empathy and was quiet. When he spoke, he was frank with his words, which were often harsh and unwelcoming. Never sugar coating to make his family members feel encouraged, his frankness was both his positive and negative attribute.

On the flip side, my parents created their own American names. When I was seven, I found out—to my shock—that my mom had an American name. She, too, wanted to fit in.

"How many members in your party?" asked the hostess at Carnations Restaurant in Los Angeles.

"Pour," my mom said, holding up four fingers.

"What is your name?" the hostess said.

"Heren," she said.

"Helen?" the hostess responded.

"Eh, yes, eh."

I looked up at my mom with surprise. Where in the world did she get the name Helen? Was it because I recently read a book about Helen Keller? As we waited to be seated, I asked.

"*Wae* (why) did you say your name was Helen?"

21

"My name starts with an *H* in Korean so I chose Helen," she shrugged her shoulders. "Helen pour Heran," my mom concluded in English. I thought about her logic.

"Then, *Umma* (mom), why is my Korean name different from my American name? My American name is Sarai means princess, but my Korean name is Mi Kyung and means. . .wait, what does *Mi-Kyung* mean?"

"*Mi* means *aleumdaun*, beautiful, good-looking."

"I'll take that. What about *Kyung?*"

"*Kyung* means *byeoseul.*"

"Uh, what? Beasoul?"

Mom pulled out her Chinese, Korean, and English dictionary and showed me the Chinese symbol for kyung and its meaning.

"Lord and sir. I'm a lord? Awesome! I'm a beautiful and powerful princess who has authority!"

"*Aigoo*, you Sarai." She smiled at me. The hostess came to take us to our seat.

"*Umma*, what about Dad?" I asked as soon as we were seated. "Does *appa* have an American name?"

"Yes, he does. He received his name when he first came to America."

"Really?" Frank interjected. "I didn't know that."

"*Eomeoni*, what is it?" Janice asked. In my sister's young childhood years, she used *jondaemal,* the honorific formal Korean form to address Mom because she wanted to honor our parents. Me? I honored them by using *banmal*, the informal, non-honorific form as a gesture to strengthen my close relationship with my parents. If I used *jondaemal,* I felt distant from my parents, whereas speaking *banmal* made me closer to them. But when I used *banmal* to other Korean adults, I was considered rude and inappropriate and was often scolded by them. However, as soon as I continued to speak in Korean, they realized my Korean language skills, an odd mixture of English, Korean, and some made-up Korean words, were poor.

Because of this, I eventually got away with speaking in *banmal.*

"Yeah, *Umma*. What is it? Tell me," I repeated.

"His name is James," my mom said.

"James? I thought it was like Manny for many because he brings home many things."

"But I thought he only brought $200 to America. That's not many," I wondered aloud. What my mom said didn't make sense, so I decided to ask my father at dinner that night.

"*Appa*," I flopped into the chair next to him. "How did you get your name, James?" Tonight, we had *kimchi* soup, rice, and seven side dishes (*banchans*). Different *banchans* glistened in the middle of the table: seasoned spinach salad (*sigeumchi namul*), little fishies (*myulchi bokkeum),* seasoned bean sprouts (*namul-muchim*), seasoned tofu (*dubu buchim*), *kimchi*, boiled beef in soy sauce (*sogogi jang jorim*) and stir-fried fish cake (*oh dang bok-kum*).

"James popular," he said. He put a piece of tofu in his mouth.

"Well, I thought it would be like Manny because you work in LA and you somehow get many things," I stated.

"I created my name at the *pyechajang* one day," he said.

"*Geugeo moya* (what's that mean)?" I asked in poor Korean grammar with a spoonful of rice in my mouth. Mom stared at me because she was teaching me to not talk with food in my mouth. I don't know why she insisted on this when dad ate and spoke with food in his mouth all the time.

"P*yechajang*," he quickly said, shoving a spoonful of rice and *kimchi* soup in his mouth.

"*Cha Jang*?" I asked, taking a chopstick-full of *myulchi*. "You used to own a Chinese restaurant and make *Cha Jang myun*?" *Chajangmyun* is noodles with black bean sauce.

"He said, *pyechajang*, which means junkyard," Janice said, shaking her head at me.

"Junkyard?" My chopsticks froze mid-air. That's right. I'm the junk baby.

"Do people come to America to work at a junkyard?" I asked Dad.

"No, many people have different jobs when they come to America," he said.

"Then why do Korean people have many businesses and drive nice cars?"

"Korean people had to work and sacrifice a lot to live in America. Some people do well, and some people do not. Sometimes, what you see is not what you really see," he said.

"Dad, tell me a little bit more about your name and your *chajang* story." I was eager to hear, so that I could have something to tell people when they asked me about my family.

"I will tell you tomorrow," he said as he took his last bite of rice. It was 8 o'clock and time for the Korean news. Dad unceremoniously left the table to turn on the television as my siblings and mom put away the dishes and leftover *banchan*. I don't know who determines cultural norms, but I did not like when only the ladies had to clean up. However, I kept my mouth shut about this.

The next night, Dad came home early. I was excited to hear the rest of his junkyard story.

"*Appa*, remember, you were going to tell me about your junk story?"

We again sat at the kitchen table, my father and I. Tonight for dinner was *doenjang jjigae* with *banchans* and *galbi*. *Doenjang jjigae* is a soybean paste soup made with fermented soybeans as a soup base with squash, onions, mushrooms, and tofu. For *banchan*, mom made homemade *kimchi* and seasoned squash. On the side, she made *galbi,* the most delectable seasoned beef. I could smell the *galbi* and imagined tiny galbi molecules floating in the air and into my nostrils. She cleaned some lettuce and scooped some *doenjang* paste onto a mini-plate with *gochu*, which is hot green peppers. Mom brought the dishes to the table for us. Janice set the utensils while Frank sat silently sat at the table. I got each of us a cup of water as my contribution to setting up the table, and sat down as well, asking Dad questions and listening.

"Well, I started to work for your uncle. Minimum wage was about $2 an hour," he said, as he took a spoonful of *doenjang jjigae*. "*Aju massiseo*," he said, declaring his verdict that the food was delicious. He took the lettuce called *sangchu* and put a piece of *galbi* and *daengjjang* sauce on the lettuce. He wrapped the lettuce like a taco, put it into his mouth, and continued his story. He tended to talk when there was food in his mouth. It wasn't attractive, and this may be the reason why Mom told me to eat and then speak.

"I didn't work that long at the junkyard. I raised some money to go back to Korea to marry your mom and bring her here."

My parents' marriage was set up in the usual "meetings." In Korea, girls bring their girlfriends, and guys would bring their boyfriends. They would meet at a coffee shop and decide who was interested in whom. Mom was pretty in a traditional way. She was not skinny like the usual pop stars; she had some meat on her body. Dad, on the other hand, was a skinny guy. No matter how much he exercised or ate, he had the DNA that would never make him gain weight. At that time, my mom's male friend introduced them. Within six months of dating and writing letters to and from Korea and America, they got married.

After marrying Mom, Dad left the junkyard job to start a business. He bought a gas station on Crenshaw Boulevard. Somehow, he was able to run a gas business with his minimal English skills, determined to make something out of himself. The 70s and 80s were eras of opportunity, and he took advantage of them. Dad was born to dabble in many things. Although he owned his own business, we were neither rich nor poor. We had good times and we had some poor times, but despite the financial roller coasters, we always had food to eat. We still had dinner together.

"I came to America because I wanted to own a business," he told me again some time later.

"You could have owned a business back in Korea. Why here?" I asked while I daydreamed of the life I could have lived in Korea. Dad's face looked worn out from a long day's work at his business. Mom, a stay-at-home mom out of choice and obligation, looked worn out, too. The daily toils of living in America, earning an income, and raising three children must have been quite difficult.

"Well, life in Korea during my time was very difficult. We believed America would be a great place to start a new life," he said. He reminisced about his past experience in Korea, sharing his life with us. Perhaps his past life in Korea was better than the current one in America. He never said.

"I was a Lieutenant and taught all the Korean soldiers Tae Kwon Do," he once told me. His eyes glittered with happiness.

"No, you didn't. You're too scrawny," I said, laughing at him. He was a short, skinny Korean man. I wondered how a scrawny Korean man could train Korean soldiers.

25

"Yes, it's true," Mom chimed in as she was making dinner for us.

"What about you, Mom? What did you do before you came to America?"

"I was a home economics teacher. I taught students the traditional foods of the kingdom era. I used to make royal foods."

"Is that why Korean food tastes so *massiso* (delicious)? *Umma*, why don't you teach in America?" I asked her in Konglish. Mom did not know how to speak English. She stayed at home because she didn't know how to communicate with non-Koreans.

Until I found out about her teaching experience, I didn't know why Mom would have me watch her prepare food. I would rather play outside, but she would call me into the kitchen to observe her. She would show me the types of ingredients that would go into making soups and preparing dishes. "How much sesame oil do you put?" I would ask. She never used a measuring cup.

"Just like this," she would say. She said knowing comes from the heart and that when I was old enough, I would know, too. I still don't know how much.

Back at the table, I listened to my dad talk about his olden days and why life was hard in Korea even though looked worn out in America.

"When I was younger," he would repeat himself at almost every meal, "we were so poor we didn't have enough food and clothing. We even walked five miles a day to and from school. We studied hard because our brains were going to get us out of poverty."

"Our family was the only family in the town who went to college," he would continue. "Everyone else didn't go. Even though we were educated, we were very poor. I was the youngest, so I didn't get to eat rice. I got leftovers from everyone else and, sometimes, I got rice water."

Maybe this was the reason why he looked so scrawny and short. On my dad's side, the males in his family were very tall. I think the males were around six feet tall. My dad was five feet five inches, give or take a couple centimeters. Perhaps the older siblings had their fill before giving my dad the leftovers.

I would listen to his stories because I enjoyed them. As I grew older, I found myself rolling my eyes because I had heard his stories a million times a million during all those dinners. I think my attitude was due to the fact that we were "privileged" to have enough food to eat and have a fairly new Mercedes Benz 450 SEL to take us to school. I wasn't sure how my dad was able to afford not one, but two luxury cars even though we were not rich.

"Make sure you finish everything on your plate," Dad always reminded us. My siblings and I had to finish our entire plates because that one kernel of rice meant a lot to him. Almost every night, I was too full to finish my plate. I couldn't eat anymore, plus my stomach hurt. I, too, was scrawny and short, always the shortest person in my class.

One day I got up without finishing my rice.

"*Bap da meoggo*! (Finish your rice!)" He bellowed. He was stern with his words, but I could see his eyes getting watery. What was wrong with him?

"You don't know what it is like to be hungry."

I looked at the two grains of rice in my bowl. It was only two grains of rice! Why was he upset? Did he have a hard day at work?

"*Nae baega ap-poh*." With my poor Korean skills, I informed my dad that my stomach hurt. "There's practically nothing left in the bowl, and I'm full."

"*Bap da meoggo!*" He elevated his voice even more. Was it because of the rice or because I didn't use honorific form to speak to my dad? At the time, I thought he was acting irrational. I needed to stand up for myself.

"This is not Korea! You are not poor anymore!" I yelled at him. At this, my father started roaring about my lack of respect for elders. In the Korean culture, I was not supposed to talk back to elders.

My dad sometimes thought we were poor, and so we needed to eat every grain of rice; but other times, we lived life as though we were rich, riding around in two Mercedes Benzes. Our external rich lifestyle was evident when we were around people, especially other Koreans. We had to appear as if we were put together and in need of no help. Whether we had money or our balance was empty in our bank account or the cash running low under my parent's mattress, my parents didn't want to be like beggars. They said we didn't need to tell people we had financial, personal, and other problems. We couldn't show any weakness in ourselves. We had to save face with people, especially other Korean people we did not know on a personal level. Even when we went to church, we had to be our very best. We were sinners who needed Jesus, but we held our head high as if we didn't have any problems.

My dad said this was Korean pride, but I wasn't sure. What I knew was that our family didn't want to be vulnerable and share with people what was really going on in our lives on a deep, human level.

The Two-Grains-Rice Day sparked a rebellion and disrespect for my parents. My siblings and I often argued with my dad. When I became a young teenager with my own personal issues on top of my dad's silly request to eat every grain in the bowl, it was just too much to take, and I would rebel even harder against my dad. My attitude stemmed from two grains of rice in my bowl or deep, hidden pain I experienced at school, classmates, and home.

As a young person, I couldn't fathom the struggles he had lived with while growing up in Korea during and after the Korean War. I guess those two grains of rice meant a lot to him. One grain of rice could have been his breakfast and the other his dinner. Growing up, I also couldn't understand the struggles my parents had lived with while their children were growing up in America.

As an adult, I did come to understand. The family arguments were much deeper than our rice wars. When Dad got upset with me, his verbal responses and treatment of me stemmed from the hidden issues that had accumulated from his wartime hunger and pain. His past was never fully healed, and my family and I received the effects of his fears, which were then regurgitated into our issues. This was a battle that I had to overcome—to fight against receiving my dad's sorrow as if it were mine. But one thing he taught was, despite all hardships, to never give up. For my dad, as the head of the household, family meant sacrificing for others, and the rice in my bowl was love and sacrifice for us.

Happy Travels

My mom, who loved buying Italian furniture and other expensive furnishings for our home, gave up when her expensive rugs, sofas, and other household items were chipped, ripped, and scratched. My siblings and I couldn't help it though. We had too much fun playing games.

In our early years, my siblings and I played games, such as Simon Says, Red Light Green Light, and Hide-and-Seek. My sister was the oldest, and most of the time, she was the ring leader who initiated the games. We complied with her commands and rules. As time progressed, rather than continuing to play with us, my sister transitioned into spending time reading books. Janice was an avid reader, and she loved reading *Sweet Valley High* book series and other books. For long periods of time, her eyes would be glued to her books. Trying to follow in her footsteps, I also read the *Sweet Valley Twins* book series. Yet, reading wasn't fun because I wasn't able to be physically active.

Since I was a year apart from my brother, I spent most of my time playing with him, whether building fortresses with the bed sheets, using green soldiers to fight against each other, or playing with action figures, such as Voltron, Transformers, and GI Joe. When my family moved to the Westside, Mom allowed us to play outside, a different experience than when we lived in the other part of Los Angeles. My brother and I played roller hockey, handball, and other outdoor games.

I wanted to take risks. On the weekends, our local friends, my brother, and I would enter our elementary school and climb the roof. Sometimes, we climbed a particular roof at school and jumped off from it with our rollerblades. We also jumped off many stairs with our rollerblades throughout the neighborhood, and when the streets were less busy, we rollerbladed down steep hills. At first, my brother was afraid because he wouldn't challenge himself to do stunts with his rollerblades, but he eventually overcame his fears.

In addition to playing indoors and outdoors with my siblings, we also went on family trips.

"Get packed!" Dad said.

"WOOHOO!" We all yelled for joy. It was our annual family trip to eat crab at Redondo Beach. Redondo Beach, along with Santa Barbara, Glen Ivy Hot Springs, the beach, and occasionally a camp site were places my family vacationed when I was in elementary school.

When we went to Santa Barbara, we stayed at the hotel with a lion statue, swam in the ocean and hotel's swimming pool, rode the surrey bike as a family, and spent quality time with each other. When we went to the hot springs, Mom put clay on her body, Janice swam at the deep end of the lap pool with Dad, and Frank and I swam in the shallow lounge pool. Sometimes, I would swim at the lap pool but hold onto the side railings just in case I got tired.

At Redondo Beach, my siblings and I went under the pier, shoveled the wet sand with our bare hands, and waited for baby crabs to emerge to the surface.

"Look!" my brother said. He found little crabs. I came over to him, leaned over, and began digging the sand near him.

"Hahaha!" We laughed at the tiny crabs that tried to crawl back inside the sand.

"Here are some crabs," my sister stated. I went over to Janice and helped her find more tiny critters.

Searching for crabs with my siblings was fun, but it was short lived. We couldn't eat the baby crabs or take them home, so we let them go. Then, it was time to eat big crabs. We headed to the north end of the pier.

As Mom and my siblings found a place to eat, Dad ordered us four crabs, since I couldn't eat a whole crab by myself. Mom ripped the legs apart and gave it to us children. She then ripped open the crab body. Dad was smiling.

"*Jeil mas-iss-da!*" Dad showed us the brown crab juice and drank it as if it were delicious. It looked like diarrhea, something not worth drinking.

Frank hammered the crab claw, showed us the chunk of meat, and took a big bite. Janice tapped her crab legs to avoid having tiny shells fly in different directions.

"Stop it!" Janice and Frank turned towards me and barked at me. I had hammered the crab leg and squirted juice at their faces.

"Sorry. I didn't mean to. It just squirts wherever it wants to." Despite the juices spurting in different directions and my siblings staring at me for not being careful when I hit the crab legs, sharing a meal with my family outside of home was the best time. Dad took time off from work, Mom didn't have to cook us food, and my siblings and I played outside.

After eating, we climbed on the rocks along the shore. Janice and Frank were careful walking on the large rocks, but I didn't mind. I hopped and skipped on the rocks.

"Be careful! Slow down." Mom said to me.

She was often worried and thought that climbing rocks, climbing walls and trees, swinging backwards on the bar rails, jumping off of many stairs, and other monkeyish activities were dangerous.

"Don't worry! I'm okay," I responded.

After climbing the rocks, sometimes, when Dad let us, we went to the arcade and played games at the pier. Playing games was most fun.

"Step right up!" The water gun game man said. "Get the water in the clown's mouth, pop the balloon, and you win!"

"Can we play?" I asked Dad. Adrenaline had kicked in, making it difficult to contain my excitement. Janice and Frank looked at Dad.

"Can we?" We all stated. Dad nodded and paid for us.

Janice sat to my left and Frank sat to my right. We held on tightly to our toy gun, slightly shaking with excitement.

"Are you ready?" The water gun game man stated.

"Yes!" We yelled. I pushed my glasses closer to my eyes, closed my left eye, and aimed the gun at the clown's mouth ready to shoot the water when the bell went off.

When the bell rang, water came out of our guns. My aim was slightly off, and I wasn't able to directly place the water in the clown's mouth. My balloon was not filling with air, so I looked to my left and right, and both my siblings' balloons were bigger than mine. Trying to catch up and fill my balloon so it would pop, the bell rang. Thinking one of my siblings had won, we turned to our side and noticed a little child, smaller than I, sitting on the other end. He had won. I think he cheated though, because his father was holding onto the gun.

After our loss, we played a few more games at the arcade, including a horse racing game and Skee-ball. The crab legs mixed with my excitement to play games gave me endless energy. Before my energy expended, Dad had told us we were done playing. I wasn't, and I told him, but he said we couldn't play more. Feeling rather upset for not being allowed to play all the games, we walked out.

"Next time," Dad said.

The next time we went on a family trip, I was 10, and we went to Santa Barbara. I had always been hesitant whenever we had gone to Santa Barbara because I held onto past pain, and controlling my emotions was nearly impossible. Crying and being angry every year were my outwards signs of frustration because I stood shy of the minimum height requirement to pedal the red surrey bike. The rental owners told me I wasn't tall enough to pedal, so I had to sit on the left side of the surrey bike, barely touching the pedal.

"Maybe next year," the rental man would say.

"I want to pedal!" I'd cry the entire time while sitting the front basket of the surrey bike.

"Well, you can't because you can't reach the pedal. We don't want you getting caught, falling, or hurting yourself."

"I won't. I can pedal standing up."

"Maybe you'll grow next year."

My brother was able to touch the pedals, but I couldn't. As the active female daughter who had learned how to swim, run fast, rollerblade, ride a bicycle, and do many outdoor activities before my brother, I was tinier than he so I couldn't pedal the surrey bike. Whether my short stature was due to eating too many candies or a Korean female gene, the supposedly fun family moments in Santa Barbara were compromised whenever I was told to sit in the front basket or in the middle between the two peddlers.

But when Dad said to get packed the year my age hit the double digits, energy surged throughout my body. I ran to the full-length mirror behind the bathroom, stood erect, and told myself I was a big girl now, ready to be measured. Yes, it was time.

We went to the bike rental station. As Dad paid for the surrey bike rental, I bent down, pumped my Reebok high-top sneakers with air, and then tilted my head towards the counter. The owner peered at me and asked me to stand next to the measuring stand. Telling myself to not tear up because I was a big girl, I walked over to the stand, slightly lifting my heel, just in case I didn't reach the red line. It worked. He said I could peddle.

"I don't think you will have the strength to peddle because you are so little," the bike rental man commented. He didn't know my prowess. Ignoring him, I sat on the left side of the surrey bike, ready to pedal.

To my parents, peddling the entire family on the bike may have been tiring, but for me, I was willing to do the hard labor because it meant I grew. The crying stopped, the frown disappeared, and the sides of my lips curled up. My heart fluttered as the Santa Barbara winds gently caressed my face, while the sweat drops emerged out of my pores. From the day I began peddling the surrey bikes, all of my family trips became fun because I got to do all the activities like the tall people.

The peddling of the surrey bike in Santa Barbara and our many family trips stopped when my sister went to junior high. We stopped playing at the arcades, climbing the rocks along the pier, or searching for baby crabs under the pier.

Now, our yearly family trips consist of driving down to Redondo Beach to silently eat crabs. We don't eat crabs on the north end anymore, but instead we go to *Hankook Hwe-Jip* (Pacific Fish Center and Restaurant) and eat king crabs and *maeuntang* (spicy seafood soup). When I hold onto the crab legs ready to hammer the shell, my siblings warn me not to squirt them. I cover the crab with a napkin. My brother shows us the meat on his crab claw, and my now vegan sister sits quietly, glaring at us for eating a formerly living and animated creature.

As we aged, I suppose our excitement for travel and play evolved. My sister enjoys spending time by herself, reading great novels and drawing. My brother creatively searches for unanswered problems as a physicist, and I continually yearn to play arcade games and be physically active even though my body and schedule prevent me from doing so. One day, when I have a family of my own, I will bring back the happy travels, passing on the tradition while creating new memories.

Working in the Hood

My dad's first business was a gas station in South Central LA on Crenshaw Boulevard. His clientele were mainly Latinos and African Americans. Although someone shot one of his workers, and several others robbed the store a few times, as a child who didn't understand the permanence of death, the crimes didn't bother me. As long as they didn't steal my candy, I was happy. I picked out any goodies I chose to eat, sometimes saving some for later. Yes, my dad's store was my store, and it was my heaven.

Unfortunately, he sold it in 1991. At the time, I was sad because it meant no more candies and chocolates. Looking back, it was a good idea that he sold it. No one suspected that the LA Riots would happen a year later and that my dad's former gas station would be set on fire. Watching on television, I wasn't even sure that what my eyes saw on the screen was real. I grew up on those streets and couldn't believe that my former neighbors would damage property and steal.

Although my dad had sold that gas station before the riots, he had a different store in LA when the riots broke out.

"Don't worry," he had reassured me. "I paid a homeless guy $100 so he would watch my store."

Well, that $100 didn't go too far; I suppose the amount wasn't enough because one of the two buildings on my father's lot still burned down. Till this day, we suffer our economic loss.

I knew the riots began with the unjust beating of Rodney King, but I didn't understand how the looters and rioters could justify the damage and violence they did. How could one person's unjust experience lead to more acts of injustice towards their own community and other ethnic groups?

Blacks, Latinos, Asians, and more lived in LA together. There were many invisible lines that demarcated us, and we tenuously lived and did business together. Different racial and ethnic groups demonstrated internal and external pain, anger, and hurt by giving each other subtle stares or making derogatory remarks and insults. African Americans made racial comments to Koreans; Koreans peered at Latinos and African Americans fearing

35

that they might steal; Africans Americans told Asians and Latinos to go back to their country. Despite conducting business together, there was anxiety, fear, and no real restorative peace. All of these tensions seemed to explode in the fires and riots that year.

As young as I was, I knew everyone was at fault. There was no justification for what had happened. We were all human beings struggling to make the best of what life had to offer, minorities who were fighting and competing with each other rather than helping each other. I wished for peace among different racial groups and equality for all, but I wasn't educated and didn't have the power to do anything about it. I just knew we needed healing.

We were one of the many owners who lost a part of their American dream in those six days. There was sadness in the atmosphere–and it wasn't just the riots. Many people were in pain, including our family.

Despite our economic struggles, my father did not let the loss of one building affect him. He got up, cleaned up the mess, and continued to work with the African American community. He was my king who demonstrated how we could still get along despite surface differences.

Later that same year, my dad's store had made a lot of money in one day. This was not the norm. As a small business owner, we didn't know when we would have money because it depended on how many customers came to my dad's store. This particular day, my dad made thousands of dollars. A high number of people had come in and out of his store that day, and the neighborhood saw. People could smell money.

That night, Mom reminded me to greet Dad at the door, like my siblings and I did every night. But Dad did not come home at his usual time, 6 pm. And he didn't come by 7 pm. At 9 pm, my siblings went to bed, and I continued to wait. I continued to wait until it was past 11 pm. Half asleep, I couldn't help but wonder where he was and why he wasn't coming home. Then I heard the door close. The hallway was dark, and he was slowly coming towards the well-lit living room. He was limping, and he didn't say much.

"Hi Dad. Did you just come?" I put on my glasses to see him better, expecting an energetic response, despite a long and tiring day. But today was different. He didn't respond at all.

As soon as he stepped into the light, I saw his discolored, bruised, and swollen face. His body bent forward as he limped and sat on the kitchen chair. His body was mangled. When we took him to the hospital later, we found that he had a fractured rib and other injuries.

He didn't cry in front of me. He may have felt ashamed. Mom found medicine in the cabinet and gently put ointment and bandages on him. I hated to see him like that.

"How did this happen?" I asked.

"I was closing up the store and was about to put the alarm on," he began, "when someone took out a gun and another person had a knife. There was a group of people with them." What could he do? His fake gun was in his suitcase. He had no weapon nor the physical prowess to protect himself. But, what happened to his Tae Kwon Do kicks and punches? In the movies, Bruce Lee fought a handful of people. My dad–a third degree black belt–didn't punch or kick anyone.

"Dad," I asked. "Why didn't you use your Tae Kwon Do skills?"

"I didn't want to die. . . Who was going to take care of the family?" he said. "What would happen if I wasn't here?"

I don't know what my life would have been like if he were gone. He said he would rather lose that chunk of money than die. He gave his wad of cash without a fight. After my dad handed over the money, those guys were still unsatisfied. Instead of simply leaving with the cash, they unleashed their desperation and anger on my dad and left him on the floor. My king was beaten alive. But, no one saw this king get beat, and if they did, no one helped him.

My king was robbed and beaten at gunpoint many times while living and working in the city. Our family began to financially suffer, but I was glad that every time, my king chose to live.

My dad still works at the same location. When I go to his store, I see the empty lot and am reminded of this sad part of LA's history – the Rodney King beating, the Riots, and my dad's beating. I see the cement floor where the building once was and tear up, hoping to find the healing that we all need.

My Home,
My Communities

"I like the number three," I shared with Mom on a quiet one-on-one meeting with her during my thirties.

"Why?"

"Well, it takes me three times to learn from my mistakes, three confirmations to make a final decision, and three children to stop having more children in our family. To top it off, we moved to three different regions and for three reasons: money, education, and environment."

"Three indeed. Maybe you need to date three different men before you meet your husband."

"*Umma*!"

From the time I was 5 years old to about 11 years old, I lived among African Americans and Latinos and attended a predominantly Latino and African American school. Most of my neighbors were black and my friends were Latino, black, Pacific Islanders, and white. The white students, along with others, came from the foster care system; at the time, I didn't know what that meant. To my recollection, my family was the only Korean family in my hood. In a patchwork county like LA, I didn't grow up thinking my neighborhood was crime-ridden, nor did I think differently about my multi-colored friends.

At night, the cops would drive by my hood. One night, I saw four cop cars surround an apartment across the street. I thought the cops were doing their duty by protecting my neighborhood.

"Mom, look at the cops across the street!" I exclaimed to Mom while peering through the glass windows from the second floor.

"Wow! This is a safe area," I thought to myself.

"Stop staring," Mom said. She came over to me and shut the blinds. "Don't see what is going on outside. Concentrate on what you need to do."

My childhood perception of my neighborhood was something I had to come to terms with as I got older and left to live in a different city. I had believed I lived in a protective community only to find out that I was living in a "dangerous" community. But really, my neighborhood wasn't even that bad. The only crimes that were committed in my neighborhood were the bikes that were stolen from my front yard, my two bunnies that mysteriously disappeared from my backyard, and the attempt to drive my parents' car as a six-year old girl (I got as far as hitting the car behind me).

My parents told my siblings and me to not play outside because of the dangerous people on the streets, but we did anyway. We especially had trouble following this rule when we wanted candy. The local liquor store was two blocks away from us, and the ice cream store was five. When our parents were not home, my siblings and I would go on a little journey to get some candy.

Money was not difficult to find. Our bank was the washer and dryer machines that Dad rented to the apartment he owned. On top of my family's stove was a small cabinet where Dad hid all his spare keys. Though I was the shortest, I was the year of the monkey, and climbing was not an issue. Using my acrobatic skills, I hopped on top of the stove and pulled out the keys as my siblings cheered me on. Janice was the one to unlock the washer and dryer and pull out some quarters. Frank was a bystander, but in any case, he would be to blame if our parents found out.

After hitting the jackpot, the three of us headed to the store to buy some candy. I really liked Now-N-Later, Taffy, Sweet Tarts, M&Ms, and . . . oh goodness, I think I just liked it all. I often chose candy and junk food over anything nutritious during elementary school, which may have been the reason for my malnourished, tiny body. Every year, I was the shortest student in my class.

During our secret trips to the liquor store, the owner and other people who stood outside stared at us. Though short and tiny for my age, barely reaching three feet tall, I always felt protected. Janice was two heads taller than I, and Frank was a head taller. My posse was with me.

Besides telling us not to play outside, Mom continuously warned us to not walk out on the streets. We wanted to obey Mom, so one day we decided to ride our bikes and scooters.

That day, the weather was warm outside. We came up around

the corner and before I knew it, two, big, black Doberman pin-schers almost as tall as I came running towards us. They were my next-door neighbor's dogs—large, ferocious monsters that barked very loudly—and we had always been afraid of them.

We immediately dropped our bikes and scooters and ran back home as fast as we could. I thought I was a fast runner, but both of my siblings got home before me and locked the door without letting me in. They refused to open the door, abandoning me to the dangerous dogs.

I first tried to protect myself by standing between the screen door and the actual door, yelling and screaming at my siblings to open the arched, wooden, castle door. The dogs were pawing their way in through the screen door. I ran out from behind the flimsy screen door, thinking I could dodge them, but soon enough the two monsters jumped me.

"Janice! Open the door! Help! Frank!" I screamed, pleading for my life while burning with anger because my siblings left me to suffer. My siblings just watched, scared, refusing to open the door.

I was scared, very scared. These ferocious dogs smelled my fear. One was in front of me and the other was behind me. Right then I promised myself that I wouldn't walk or ride my bike in the neighborhood anymore. Mom was right.

The dog in the front smelled my neck area, and both of the dogs put their paws on my front and backside. I was trapped. The monstrous dogs then leaned over, exposing their teeth, and licked me. For the next ten years, I had a phobia of dogs, and every time I saw a big, black dog, I was reminded of being trapped between two pairs of monstrous paws and yellow teeth.

My neighborhood *was* dangerous. More than guns and po-lice, these giant dogs were the most terrifying. After that, I stayed inside like my mom told me.

As time went on, my parents decided it would be best to move to a new community, out of the heart of LA. Our family moved to the Westside–it was a short-lived, fun time. We moved into a new middle class community where people owned homes–some three bedrooms while others were very big.

My brother and I attended the local elementary school, and my sister went to the nearby junior high school, a major reason for our move. Since it was "safe," my mom said we were allowed to play outside. I made some friends, who were mostly white and Persian, and two Asians. However, in the sixth grade, I befriended my amigos. A handful of Latino friends were bussed in every day from LA. Bussing students out of the area was new for the school and for me. When a few Latino students arrived to my class, the teacher told one of them to sit next to me. He quickly sat down and was quiet. He put his book bag on the side of the desk, sat straight, and crossed his hands. He was wearing a grey suit with an ironed white dress shirt.

"Hi, I'm Sarai," I said.

"I'm Julio. I'm from LA."

We quickly became friends. He was my school partner, very smart, and always well-dressed in suits and slacks. One big bonus was that he was shorter than I. Throughout the year, he and I would measure who was taller. He definitely cheated because he had hair that went straight up, and the teacher counted his hair as part of his height. For class pictures, we lined up according to height, so I was always the last student.

Despite our height wars and school camaraderie, Julio and I never spent time together outside of class. After school, Julio was bussed back to his neighborhood; he was a stranger living in the rustling and chaotic sounds of East Los Angeles. But at school, in the quiet suburbs of green front lawns, he was my friend.

After a couple of years, my parents decided to move to the edge of LA–opposite from the Westside after my first semester of 7th grade.

"Where are you going?" Jazzy and Anne asked me. They were my two Asian friends, Chinese and Japanese, besides my Middle Eastern, African American, White, and Latino friends.

"Seh-lee-tos. That's what my mom told me."

"Cerritos?"

"No, my mom said it's far, and it's in Seh-lee-tos."

Forgetting my mom had a thick Korean accent, I soon discovered that my friends were right; we moved to Cerritos. Leaving behind friends and memories distressed me because I was not only moving into my new home, but also transitioning out of my prepubescent stage and searching to form my identity. My multicolored family – Persians, African Americans, Latinos, and white friends–disappeared, and I was left with Asian faces surrounding me. Seeing a high percentage of Asians gave me culture shock. My new school, where groups segregated by race, was overwhelming and confusing. At first, I didn't know who I was or where I could find black and Latino friends. People hung out with their own "kind." The Asians hung out with each other. The whites hung out with each other. The blacks hung out with each other. The Latinos hung out with each other. Then again, there weren't many Latinos. Where did they hang out? Which group was I supposed to join? In my old communities, we would all hang out together. But it was different here. Friendships were difficult to cultivate despite our Asian similarities, and it was not until Angel, a Korean girl–my first Korean friend in the city–asked me to join her group that I had any friends.

While I lived in Cerritos, I informed people that I was there temporarily, and that I was from the heart of LA. However, when I went to San Diego for college and people asked me where I was from, I said, "Cerritos." Without my being aware of it, this Asian-infested city and surrounding communities where I grew up during my adolescent years had become my home.

PART 2

BIBIMBAP AND BANCHAN

Bibimbap is mixed rice, and banchans are small side dishes of food served with rice.

Bibimbap and Banchan

Korean foods typically have not only main dishes but also a variety of *banchans*. The number of these side dishes placed on the table may range depending on the particular occasion or the cook's preference. *Banchans* may consist of sprouts, cucumbers, leafy greens, seafood, glass noodles, roots, *kimchi*, sweet beef, spicy fish, saucy potato, fish cakes, rice cakes, and more. They come in many flavors, spices, and intensity, and the flavors can be sweet, salty, bland, and umami.

At home or at a Korean restaurant, *banchans* are placed in the center of the table for people to share. They are in small plates and in small portions. When a particular *banchan* is limited, mom at home or the *unnies* ("older sisters"–Korean waitresses) at a Korean restaurant would refill it. Going to a Korean restaurant was a blessing because the *banchans* were free and never ending. *Banchans* usually came out first, and then soup (*guk*), and then other items along with rice bowls. However, sharing *banchans* also meant sharing other people's germs. As people put their chopsticks in their mouths, they would take it out and pick up the same or different *banchan* from the middle of the table. By the time a meal was finished, everyone's saliva was intermingled. Hopefully, the people at the table were family or close friends, and if they were strangers, we became family at the end of the meal.

Many non-Korean parents expressed that their children had a difficult time eating vegetables. But in my home, this was not a problem. Korean *banchans* were an approach to eating a variety of vegetables. I've come to appreciate the *namul banchans*, which are an assortment of different vegetables that have been marinated, boiled, steamed, or stir-fried with different seasonings, such as sesame oil, salt, garlic, and chili peppers. Broccoli, spinach, sprouts, cucumber, carrots, and radishes were vegetables I enjoyed eating at a age.

My two favorite *banchans* were *jang-jorim* and *ojingeochae bokkeum*. *Jang-jorim* is brisket beef simmered in a sweet, dark

47

brown marinade made out of soy sauce. In order to eat *jang-jorim*, mom would scoop some hot steaming rice into a bowl and pour water over it to make rice soup. After taking one spoonful of rice, she would then put the *jang-jorim* on top of the rice and feed me. *Ojingeochae bokkeum* is dried squid that is stir-fried and mixed with *gochujang* (chili pepper paste) and other flavorings. The best times I ate Korean food were when I had *ojingeochae bokkeum* and *jang-jorim* with rice water.

One of Korea's national and staple *banchans* is *kimchi*. It doesn't seem all too palatable because it is fermented vegetables, which produces a very distinct and strong aroma. *Kimchi* includes different vegetables such as radish, napa cabbage, and cucumber, and ranges from not spicy to very spicy. Common *kimchi* dishes are o*i-sobagi* (stuffed cucumber kimchi), *nabak-kimchi (cabbage), kkakdugi (radish), and dongchimi* (watery radish). While the first three all make use of red chili pepper flakes for spiciness, *dongchimi* is sweet, tart, and refreshing.

Acquiring the taste of *kimchi* began when I was three years old. Using chopsticks, mom split pieces of *kimchi* into thin strips. She would then take a piece of the *kimchi* and dip it in water to take out the red chili flakes, making it less spicy. Next, she would place the watered *kimchi* on top of my rice and feed me. Mom gradually left more and more pepper flakes on the *kimchi*, and before I knew it, I was eating real *kimchi*.

Rice and *banchan* were enough to fill me up. Although it was okay to eat only *banchan* at home, mom taught me to eat *banchans* sparingly and order some sort of meat, poultry, soup, and other dishes when we went to restaurants.

"All I need is rice and *banchan*."

"It is not good to just eat *banchan* only at a Korean restaurant without ordering dishes," she said, "we need to give them business, and it's just not right."

"I'll get *bibimbap*," Janice informed the waitress.

"Okay," I said, turning to my mom. "Can I get *yook gae jang*-the spicy beef soup?"

"It's spicy," Mom remarked.

"I know."

"*Unni*, she'll have the *yook gae jang.*" Mom informed the waitress. "When did you start liking so many spicy foods?" She inquired.

"When you started feeding me *kimchi*."

After we ordered, the *unni* brought out a variety of *banchans* to the table. I took out the wooden chopsticks, rubbed the sticks together to take out unwanted splinters, and began tasting all the *banchans* like the spicy cucumber *kimchi*, sweet and glazed potato, potato and fruit salad, and seasoned boiled spinach.

"Mom, how come there are so many different *banchans*?"

"I don't know. It depends on the restaurant," she answered as she tried the restaurant's *kimchi*.

"Well, wasn't your degree in home economics or something? I thought you learned how to make royal food dishes."

"Yes."

"Then, can't you tell me why there are different kinds of *banchans*?"

"Well, there are too many royal dishes. I wasn't able to learn all of them."

"Okay. How come different restaurants serve different *banchans*?"

"Because they want to," she responded without looking at me. I think she was ignoring me because she was hungry.

Her answer didn't satisfy my curiosity. "Mom, what is the meaning of *banchans*? How come Koreans are the only ones that have an assorted collection of side dishes?"

Mom let out a sigh. "I don't know. I know that *banchans* are passed down from each generation. We share what we know and transfer it to the next generation."

"Then, how come some *banchans* that are similar taste different?"

She stared at me with her "be quiet" look.

When my family and I moved to an Asian community with mostly Koreans, I began to think about the significance of having different *banchans* and why the same *banchan* made by different people tasted unique. In the beginning, I thought Koreans looked the same. However, as I began to acclimate to my new Korean community, I realized Koreans were like assorted *banchans*. We had distinct flavors, styles, spices, seasonings, and types.

Mom, Janice, and I ate a piece of the *kimchi* in the center of the table. Biting into the tangy, spicy *kimchi*, I was reminded of some Koreans. They had a kick to their words. Whether they used a calm or condescending voice, what they said was demeaning and hurtful. Their words left a kick in my heart. Mrs. Kim used to tell me I looked too skinny and like a sickly child. The way she said those words reminded me of the red peppered *kimchi* that was made with oyster. She had a smell to her comments. Then there were the bitter and salty Korean *ahjummas* who had frowning faces and complained about the little things. If the room temperature was too hot or too cold, they complained. When their husbands didn't do what they wanted them to do, they nagged. Their constant *jansoli* reverberated for many years, like sour, undigested food that never came out of their bodies. Korean *ahjusshis* were not better than their wives. They criticized and got easily upset at their nagging, miserable wives. They, too, ended up complaining and criticizing; however, they were like *napa kimchis* because they were *napo*, ungrateful men who didn't appreciate their wives.

Other people were like fish *banchan*, and they left an oily fishy smell, jagged teeth, and sharp bones wherever they went, similar to people who were sneaky or had ulterior motives. These fish embittered my soul. Other fish, such as *myulchi bokkeum*, were two-faced fish that increased my blood pressure and left piercing marks on my body as time progressed. In the beginning, I had thought the little anchovies were freshwater fish because of their sweet taste. They reminded me of people I initially met through friendships and dates. They were delightful, but after some time or when they were treated the wrong way, their boney weapons came out to jab me. These initial sweet fish were actually salty fish rinsed with water, and coated with refined sugar or honey.

While many fish *banchans* pierced my heart, *namul banchans* and *jorim banchans* strengthened and comforted me. People of great strength and courage were like the spinach in the *sigeumchi namul banchan*. These people reminded me of courageous *Weh-Halmoni,* who overcame negativity and hardships. Grabbing a handful of *sigeumchi namul* with my chopsticks, I desired to gain superhuman strength to withstand people's *jansolis* and negativities.

Besides *sigeumchi namul* banchan, the *jorim*, dishes simmered in sauce helped me subdue my rage. *Jang-jorim* banchan not only was delicious but also required time to make because the meat was cooked twice, first with water and second with soy sauce and other ingredients. The meat is first soaked in cold water and then placed in a pot to boil until it is tenderized. This process also dissolves the albumin, the stuff that can make the meat tough and hard to chew. After becoming soft, the meat is then slowly braised in a mixture of soy sauce, vegetables, spices over a medium flame for several hours. When I got upset, frustrated, or angry, cold water was used to bring my filthy thoughts and actions to the surface, and the boiled water vaporized my negativities. Water cleansed and softened the hard fibers in my heart from acting upon my destructive thoughts.

The combined sauce used to make the *jang-jorim* helped me understand that differences will always exist. People around me will not always be pleasant, like the garlic smell, peppery kick, and spoiled egg. However, when my negativities were discovered and boiled out, the vegetables and sauces in their right combination made the *jang-jorim* dish savory and worth the wait. All I had to do was take my issues out and value and accept people for their individualities.

The *unni* brought Janice her *bibimbap*—a variety of vegetables or *banchans* mixed with hot pepper paste, sesame oil, and rice. As she mixed the vegetables in the sizzling hot stone bowl, I couldn't help but think how my own life was like *bibimbap*. My friends were like the *banchans* that made my dish flavorful and colorful, a unique and satisfying blend of different cultures. Although the dish looks simple, the vegetables are prepared and seasoned to taste oh so delicious.

Whereas my sister mixed her *bibimbap* thoroughly in her *dolsot*, I took out one or two food items from my dish I didn't want to eat. Mom didn't like me picking my food because the process took too long.

"Stop picking your food." She saw me take every onion out of my *yook gae jang.* "Just eat the onions. It's good for you."

"I know, but I'm going to take it out because it makes the food taste weird and my breath smell bad."

"Once it is cooked together, it is hard to take out. The flavor is still combined."

"Maybe."

"Once you are born and you are living in the world, you can't separate yourself from your surroundings. You are already connected with the people around you, and with society."

"Well, does connection mean I need to be affected by them?" I inquired.

"You already are. From your experiences, new meanings form and you make choices in life based on your experiences and the people around you."

Janice scraped the hardened rice from the side of the *dolsot*.

Staring at my sister's *bibimbap*, I stated, "Ok, *bibimbap* is a mix, and I am a combination of many people and environments. Some things I like and others I don't."

"Correct. Learn what is good and not good and make wise choices. Though you can take out the bad *banchan* or *ka-shi* if you choose to do so, remember that your *bimbimbap* is very mixed, so a residue of those things may linger, similar to the onions that were cooked in your *yook gae jang*. That's the same with life. Memories stay with us. Just don't become bad *banchan* yourself."

My Banchan

All of my life I have understood that I was to put others before me. If there were elders, I had to serve them at all times. When there was a piece of food left on the plate, and the choice was between my siblings and me, my mom would always tell me to let them have the last bite. If it were my older sister, my mom would say I was younger, and I should give my older sister whatever she wanted first to show respect. If it were between my brother and me, my mom would say to let my younger brother have whatever he wanted first because I was his older sister. Apparently, a middle daughter's only right was to give up her rights. I often thought I was a Korean Cinderella.

One time a Korean grandma overflowed our house toilet with baby wipes. Brown chunks of poorly digested *kimchi* and leftover anchovies overflowed out of the porcelain bowl, now just a brown mess of baby wipes and feces. Mom told me to clean the bathroom because I was her special one. And my siblings? They disappeared when they discovered the work was arduous and dirty. I wasn't sure if they were punishing me for the times I didn't help them put away the food or clean my mess, but I was left alone to do the grimy work.

Church was no different. I was the submissive female who served but couldn't lead because I was not a male. The immigrant Korean church's mentality that only males could be leaders contradicted my understanding of men and women. Did they not know that I was a female – *fe*+male? *Fe* means iron, so I was an iron-male; therefore, I was much stronger than males. To my 10-year-old mind, this made perfect sense. I even had evidence of my iron-maleness: I was much stronger than most of the scrawny and awkward boys in my class. I could run faster, beat them in arm wrestling, and climb trees higher and quicker than all of them.

I then hit my teenage years, and my straight tomboy-ish features began to curve and soften. My confidence in my *Fe*+ maleness hardened into the belief that being strong meant that I needed to loudly assert my opinion on every issue, talk back to my immigrant parents, criticize them for their narrow-minded traditions, and educate everyone around me about how to fix themselves.

One evening, after a fight with my dad, who had yelled at me for not finishing my food, my mom came to talk to me. This hadn't been the first time my dad and I had fought over unfinished food on my plate.

Without asking, she opened my bedroom door, which I had loudly slammed, and sat on my bed. I didn't look at her but stubbornly kept my eyes fixed on the pink flowery pattern of my heavy silk comforter. It was the type of blanket seen in many Korean households and had been a gift for my 11th birthday, an attempt by my parents to balance out my tomboyish tendencies and make me more feminine. I hadn't thanked them for it, instead commented how I'd wanted striped cotton jersey sheets that many of my friends had.

My mom, unfazed by my silent rage, began talking.

"Women are very strong. We don't need to show how strong we are because those who do are actually weak. The strong person is the person who goes last, who lifts others forward rather than trying to climb on top of people, and who gives rather than receives."

I kept quiet, and she left.

I tried to forget her words. I purposely acted aggressively, arrogantly, and competitively, the opposite of what her words were trying to show me.

But, I couldn't forget her words. Whenever I saw the quiet strength of a classmate who was being bullied, or the immigrant Korean wife who still fed and took care of her ungrateful husband, people's jealousy fuming out of their insecurities, or even myself doing the same negative things as others, I heard my mother's words.

The older I became, the more aware I was of how people mistreated, devalued, and disregarded each other based on physical appearances, biased perceptions, skin color, status, and titled positions. I wanted to do something about it, but I first had to heal from my own wounds.

Other People's Banchans

Rich Banchan

Going to a Korean restaurant with Korean adults was entertaining when it came to paying for group meals. In Korean gatherings, one person would pay the entire bill. I didn't realize that this was not common until I went to college and people paid for themselves.

When the bill got dropped off at the table, the first person would snatch the check. My dad often grabbed the check first, which meant financial arguments between my parents at home.

"Oh, no! I need to pay for this meal," the Korean *ahjusshi* said. He was wealthiest out of the group. We all knew it.

A bald-headed, round-bellied *ahjussi* grabbed the check. "Oh no. I will pay for it." He was the cockiest out of the group. Short and stocky–and always flashy.

Deciding who was going to pay was like playing tug-o-war. Someone would grab the check, and then another person would, and then another person would. Sometimes, a person would hold on to the check but would finally "unwillingly" hand it over.

"Ha ha ha. Let me pay for it," the overweight, flat-nosed, dark-faced *ahjussi* said.

"Oh, no! I will pay for it." At this time, my dad took out his credit card and put it on the check.

Both wealthy *ahjussi* and flashy *ahjussi* shook their heads to display a slight hesitation, "Ah, I should pay for it . . . but if you insist."

Usually, the person who made the least or the most amount of money would pay. Sometimes the person who wanted to show off that he had money would pump his chest and pay for the check, and we would later find out that he had paid with his credit card and was struggling to make ends meet. A wealthy family would sometimes pay for the meal; and other times, they would have another family with less money pay for it. Though

55

different people paid for the meal, someone with a "titled position," such as a pastor from a church, would not even consider paying for the meal. They sat back, smiled, and received the meal as a gracious gift.

I was never sure if all of this bouncing around of the check was a dance of generosity or a show. For my family, it was both. We truly desired to give. In my household, actions meant love in lieu of the words, "I love you." In public, we gave and paid for people. However, at home, when times were tough, we received waves of negative ramblings of not having enough money. When money was tight, financial stress suffocated my parent's daily conversations. I didn't understand. If my parents did not have money to buy food for people or "friends," they shouldn't even offer.

"Why do you pay for people when you argue with mom at home, and we don't have a lot of money?"

"It's a gesture of love," Dad answered. "It's a Korean tradition."

"Then have other Korean people pay for us. Isn't it their tradition, too?"

Dad was silent for a moment. Then, as if he decided something, he said, "You will understand when you grow up."

"I hope so, because I really don't right now. We usually end up paying for meals. We're not rich . . . or maybe we are and you're hiding the money?"

"We are rich," Mom said.

"No and yes," Dad chimed in.

"Then, why do you talk about money all the time with Mom as if we're tight?"

"Being rich doesn't always mean having money. At times, you cannot see richness in people," Mom said.

"Yeah, but you have rich friends. They are for sure rich; I saw their homes and cars. I see their richness."

"Though we have or do not have enough money compared to the Lee's and Park's, we are very rich. That's why we bless others," stated Dad.

"Sometimes, just because people have money doesn't mean they're rich. They may live a life of emptiness that overshadows their money." Mom's words usually went skin deep.

"Yeah, but your friends. They seem to be rich on the inside and outside. Shouldn't they bless us, too? Don't we go to church with them?"

"Well, what you see is not what you really see," Dad shared. "It's better to bless others than to be blessed by others."

"Learn to understand and see people beyond what is in front of you. Then, you will understand how rich people are." Mom smiled at me.

I did eventually learn to see people's richness, regardless of their financial wealth or lack thereof. To honor their worth, I often find myself sharing food that I have packed, or paying for friends' meals and coffee.

Insecure Banchans

Many of our immigrant parents brought their childrearing traditions with them from Korea. Unfortunately, their approach often backfired. We grew up being talked down to, and some of us were physically abused. Most of all, the hidden pain came from psychological and verbal abuses. Our parents, having experienced physical and emotional abuse in their birth family, thought this was normal, so they would pass down their experiences to us. But it would feed our already vulnerable sense of self.

"*Appa*, why do you say negative words to me?"

"Because you will work harder," he often told me.

He would say things like, "You're not using your head," and "You need to eat more." He had a plethora of words to "encourage" me to work harder.

My friends, though, suffered more than I did.

"Why can't you be more like your brother?" Sarah's dad said to her.

"Are you stupid? *Babo*! Straighten up." A dad knuckled his son's head. Paul was fuming internally for feeling belittled in front of me.

"Get your act together, or you'll get a beating." Jin's body tensed as he clenched his fists. He said nothing.

Many Korean adults went around telling us to study all the time knowing and hoping that a good education would create more opportunities for us. Their way of "encouraging" us was to consistently compare us to their friends' children.

"*Gongbu! Gongbu! Gongbu!* Cho's son is going to Harvard, why can't you study more?"

Often, the nagging and "encouragement" also came from ajummas.

"You're pretty on the outside, but you are disrespectful and rude," stated the Korean *ahjummas,* who believed their age, status, and life experiences allowed them to dictate the terms of Korean American females' behavior and actions.

A lot of Korean parents were also more concerned with their children's outward appearances than what was going on with us on the inside. When a girl was ugly, they highlighted her intelligence.

If a Korean girl were pretty and smart, then they leaned towards her beauty. If the girl was not smart or was a troublemaker who gave her parents a headache, people didn't say anything. You could hear the innuendo in "Oh, your daughter is pretty" compared to "Oh, she is your daughter. She looks like she is smart." I grew up hearing too many comments about Korean girls who were not pretty enough, smart enough, or talented enough.

"You need to get your eyes done."

"Your nose is too flat."

"You look...*healthy*." Jenny bowed her head and took a sip of her black coffee to avoid looking at the *ahjummas*. Seeing that she was hurt and attempting to encourage her, the *ahjummas* continued, "Yayaya, don't worry, this can be fixed. You can drink *hanyak*, the Korean oriental medicine, to lose weight, and if you get double-eyelid surgery, then you could look pretty like your American friends, too."

Jenny's mom agreed with her friends. They sat around the kitchen table scrutinizing Jenny's body though they themselves had flat noses, *ttong baes* known as belly rolls, and small eyes. Why point fingers at us to make us feel bad when we were mirror images of them?

Despite the face-to-face criticisms, they had short moments when they were content and proud of us. This happened when Korean adults came together, especially the *ahjummas,* in public settings. The Korean ladies knew how to *jalang* about their children.

"My daughter is not too pretty, but she got all straight A's in her advanced classes. She's only in 10th grade, and she's in calculus."

"My son. I don't know what happened. All of a sudden, he wanted to start a business, and he's only in 11th grade. I don't know where he got his business skills and intelligence. He's making good money and is saving up for college."

"My daughter got accepted to an IVY League college. She is a hard worker."

"Oh, this Gucci bag? It's for Suzi. I thought it would look good on her."

"My daughter has natural double eyelids and her eyes are very big and pretty. She looks a little bit like me, right?"

I questioned why the *ahjummas* had nothing better to do but chatter nonsense and spend time boasting about their children when afterward they came home and criticized us. They were really proud of us when we demonstrated the potential to attend a prestigious college or to make a lot of money—most likely in hope of receiving that money from us as acknowledgement of the sacrifices they made for us. Most of all, they were proud when we submitted to them.

Now, I wonder if their insecurities made it impossible to love us without fear, control, or pain. Perhaps it was just too overwhelming—being immigrants, learning a new language, raising a family, giving up their own dreams to work double shifts at a blue-collar job, and on top of that trying to preserve the Korean culture that they loved. As an adult, I saw their sacrifice; I saw their love. I saw that they did the best they could.

But it still hurt.

Ka-Shi Banchan

Whenever we went to a Korean restaurant that served deep-fried or seasoned fish as a *banchan*, my mom would always warn me, "Remember to take out the *ka-shi*." *Ka-shi* were fish bones, and some tinier ones would be hidden within the hot, steaming white meat.

"What if I chew on it? What if I swallow it by accident?" I asked.

"Some *ka-shi* you can eat, but some types you have to take out," she said as she took out a hidden bone. "Like this one. This would not be good for you because it could poke holes inside your body. You won't know its pain till later. Some people have internal issues that can't be seen on the outside until it's too late. Remember to look to see if there are any hidden *ka-shi*. Once it's in, the damage starts."

She wasn't making me feel very good about eating. I thought about bones stuck in my throat and stomach lining. Painful.

"These *ka-shi* are hidden," she stated. "So be careful with the people you meet."

"Huh? People?" How did we go from talking about fish bones to people?

"Yes, the wrong and bad people will give you *ka-shi*. Sometimes what people say and do will leave big *ka-shi* inside of you."

"Ah, I see." I felt a little better about the fish once I realized this wasn't about the food.

"Make sure you avoid being around smelly fish with harmful *ka-shi*. If you experience one of these, take it out before it harms you internally."

"Okay."

As I grew up, I came to learn that what I see is not what I really see. What seemed too good to be true was a false reality. I realized there were people who have swallowed tiny *ka-shi* as well large *ka-shi*. Or they may have slowly ingested small *ka-shi* that ended up damaging them in untold ways. I saw how some of my friends lived an externally "perfect" life, but they had eaten a lot of *ka-shi* that was now hidden.

Wangstas

Ken had long bangs that dangled to the sides of his chin. He was a young 11th grade "wangsta," a wannabe gangsta, who wore baggy clothes, mostly oversized blue jeans, and a white t-shirt. He often went to *noraebangs* to drink, smoke, and sing the latest Korean songs with his fellow wangsta friends, and sometimes he got into trouble.

The wangstas created an internal hierarchy system at school. In the Korean culture, younger people bow to older people; in school, the wangstas used their status to control younger students. If the younger students didn't bow 90 degrees, then they would be beaten up, smacked around, or be punked. The older students were addicted to control and power.

To me, they weren't thugs but broken boys who lacked the communication skills to express their emotions. They either grew up without fathers, or if they had fathers, the fathers were absent from their lives. The only time their fathers knew they existed or communicated with them was to beat them up with their fists or words or both. Support and access to engage in meaningful conversations were absent. The wangstas ended up expressing their feelings through negativity, violence, and disruptive behavior. Ken was one of these boys.

When we were younger, Ken and I went to the same tutoring center. Even though I knew he was smart, schooling was painful for him. He didn't try, looked disengaged, and mainly copied people's work. Every year in elementary school, he had teacher-parent conferences for his misbehavior and poor performance.

"He's Asian, he should do well in school," teachers would say. "He has so much potential." Ken's mom, with her limited English, would smile and nod while the teacher spoke. Although she didn't know what the teacher said, she knew Ken was not doing well.

As a teenager, Ken still struggled with being a student. He had just been kicked out of his previous school after being caught with marijuana and had transferred mid-year to mine. After many years of being told he was lazy, Ken wanted to apply himself at his new school and concentrate on his studies. He had hoped that this new school would be a new start for him.

Ken was enrolled in biology class, and for his assignment, he made a poster that classified the kingdom and species of animals and plants. He was proud of his work because he actually tried and finished--on time.

When he got his poster back, he threw it on the floor. "Shit! My teacher gave me an F!"

"What? Why?!" I asked, confused. He had done phenomenal work.

"My biology teacher thought I was tagging. He said my writing was gangster writing, and he didn't want any gang affiliation written on any homework assignment. I told him I wasn't involved in any gang, and that I was making the letters more appealing." He clenched fist and punched a desk and then a wall.

"AHH! I don't want to try because when I try, I get in trouble! Why do teachers have to judge me based on my appearance and my handwriting!"

I looked at the poster and noticed the letters looked like calligraphy and not the usual bubbly writing Koreans had at school. I didn't understand why he was deemed as an Asian gangster or why his teachers misjudged him. Did they not see Ken's life potential beyond the letters, bangs, and baggy clothes?

After trying to do well in school, his experience in biology class and other classes continued him on a downward spiral. He began to spend his time with the wangstas again, laughing and punking younger students under the tree behind the cafeteria. After school hours, Ken continued to drink and smoke and sing melodramatic Korean love songs at the *noraebang*.

Among the wangstas that Ken hung out with, a senior named Jin was one who stands out the most in my memory. He was academically strong and possessed an all-around solid package that attracted many universities. He had a scholarship to a prestigious college waiting for him. But Jin's internal *ka-shi*, years of psychological and physical abuse by his parents, punctured, and eventually destroyed, his fragile future.

One day, Jin, Ken, and their "gang" decided to punk a particular group of young Korean students who wouldn't bow to them. They dragged the younger boys to a local park, beat them almost unconscious, and threw them in the trunk.

The following month, a police officer came to my math class and calmly spoke with the teacher. Her usual bubbly demeanor disappeared as she nodded. The police officer approached Jin and asked him to follow. Jin got up and strolled out of the classroom with the police officer.

Later, we heard that Jin was charged with attempted kidnapping and abuse. Just fifteen minutes of razor-edged rage ripped away all that Jin had worked for, and it ruined his future. Other wangstas were reported for their abuse as well; Ken, however, being just a bystander, was not convicted of anything.

This incident possibly left a deep mark on Ken. He began to try. He went to night school to make up his failed classes and got his high school diploma on time. Ken's parents were hoping he would make it to a 4-year college, but Ken still battled with the *ka-shi* that told him he wasn't good enough. I tried to encourage him, but he kept me at a distance.

"I don't think I'm college material. I'm gonna enlist in the army and figure out my life."

"Why don't you register at a community college?" I asked. "I think you're smart. You have potential."

"Maybe later. Lemme get my act together first and get away from home."

He wasn't very successful in the military, but it taught him to listen to authority. Ken eventually did attend a community college for four years and then received a scholarship to a 4-year university.

I ran into Ken and his wife not too long ago in LA. He looked older, and he spoke about his family and work with a blustering confidence. But in his eyes I could see the old *ka-shi,* the hidden things that could potentially disrupt his fragile life.

Little d on D

I could be at a restaurant, and across from me a little boy with spiked hair happily eats his mac and cheese. Or at school, when I desire help from a mentor, the question will pop up, "Does he have someone who can help him now?" Sometimes, I'll think of Little d when I see young boys loitering in the parking lot, a cloud of cigarette smoke blurring their half-glassy eyes. And, usually, I'll say a little prayer for Little d.

He was a young Korean boy who lived in my neighborhood. He was cute and short and had a future that could have been great. All the girls thought he was adorable. He began using hair gel when he was pretty young. He took globs of cheap green gel and made his hair look like a porcupine with spikes that were two or three inches high. I used to touch his hair because I liked the prickly feeling.

"Little d, you're so cute with your hair," I said every time he would bike over to my friend's house. He never came alone because he was too young. He came with his older Korean buddy, Paul – someone no mother would approve of. This buddy was bad. I believe Little d was in elementary school, maybe in the third grade, when his "buddy" taught him how to smoke, do drugs, steal, and get into fights.

Little d began ditching elementary school to hang out with his buddy. I wasn't sure if his parents knew. They were busy working, sometimes taking double shifts to make ends meet and put food on the table. Little d didn't have parents to take care of him after school.

This was the same for Paul. It was said that he came from a family where his mother was a gambler and his father would disappear for days when life at home got too difficult. Life in America for his parents was rough, and eventually, his dad ended up bailing on him.

Little d was a latchkey boy who hung out with the wrong friend. He probably looked for an older brother or companion to fill up time or fill the void that was inside of him. His older buddy took care of him, but it came with a price. Bad influence, drugs, cigarettes, and alcohol - the various *ka-shi* began building up in Little d's little body.

The last I heard, Little d tried robbing a store, and his picture appeared on the store's wanted list. I wish I could have been his older sister and helped him create a healthy path. However, back then, I didn't know how to.

Young and Restless

Although on the outside we often looked "normal," our hidden *ka-shi* sometimes manifested at various times when least expected. Living in an Asian-infested city and *saving face* while negotiating the American and Korean cultures was a balancing act. Life for us was tough, but our outer appearance as model students and citizens, as well as our masks that perpetuated this myth, prevented us from getting the real help we needed.

When some of my Korean friends were down, they took E, or ecstasy, and went raving in Riverside or at people's homes. When they had to study for a test and procrastinated, they popped speed. When they wanted to be cool, they drank and smoked. When they were the outcasts, they smoked pot, got into fights, vandalized buildings, or stole. When they were fat, they popped diet pills, starved themselves, and threw up. When their lives were messed up, they mixed their drugs with coke, alcohol, and other drugs. When they hated their lives, they ran away or tried to commit suicide. When they were pressured to do well in school, they cheated.

Young was 13 years old, an only child and new to our neighborhood. His immigrant parents did not graduate from college and were working menial jobs in America. Young felt the enormous weight of his parents' expectations.

Young was fearful of his dad, even though they were the same height. When his dad was in a bad mood or drunk, Young and his mother received some lashings. Young didn't talk about his parents often. At times, he joked around and smiled at school to cover up the troubles he experienced at home, but mostly he kept quiet.

At school, he hung out with his Korean and other Asian friends. After school, Young and his friends went to his house to drink and smoke. They were only in 8th grade. My girlfriends and I went to visit him and his friends occasionally because he went to my school and lived in my local neighborhood.

One Saturday morning, trying to find people to hang out with, I rollerbladed around my neighborhood. Young opened the door and let me in. He looked stressed and upset. Paul was with him, and they were smoking and drinking. Young chugged his father's beer.

"Are you okay?" I asked.

Young was looking down and angrier than I had ever seen him.

"Let him be," Paul said. "He's cooling down."

"Hey, some of us are going to be swimming later. Let me know if you want to join us."

"Shut the fuck up!" He yelled at me. I froze, shocked. He had never said profane words to me. What was up with him?

"Dude, you don't have to say that to me."

"Get out or be quiet."

I stood there and wondered what had just happened. Something had changed inside of him.

"Get out!" he yelled, and he threw a plastic chair across the room. Suddenly aware that his anger was quickly escalating to violence, I walked out of the area.

"I'm going."

As I was about to put on my rollerblades, he threw his hard rubber slipper at my head. The blow didn't really hurt as much as the shock. I'd never had anyone throw a shoe at my head nor gotten a beating from anyone, and I felt like it was about to happen. I needed to get out quick.

"Didn't I say to fucking get out!" He pushed my arm and back a few times. And then he punched my arm twice. Fear struck me. Tears rolling out of my eyes, I grabbed my rollerblades and ran out. My heart was palpitating and my entire body was shaking so badly that I stumbled as I rollerbladed home. I never went back to his place.

A couple months later, Young approached me and asked why I didn't say hi or come by and hang out with the group.

"I don't want to." Didn't he remember?

"Hey, we're going to have a pool party. Come if you can," he said.

"Dude, I don't want to get hit by you." I remarked.

"What do you mean?" Young looked confused.

I sneered at him. "What?"

"What?"

"You don't remember?"

"Remember what?"

"You yelled at me and punched me several times. You even threw something at me!" The tears began to fall.

"I don't remember. I didn't do that. Why would I hit my friend?"

"Friend or what. That wasn't cool. I don't want to be around you. You're too violent. Whatever your parents did to you, you shouldn't do it to others, especially a girl." I walked away and stopped going to that part of my neighborhood.

Due to my incident with Young, I had an ambivalent compassion for quiet, stoic-faced Korean men who drank and smoked. While I wanted to help him find solutions to their problems, I was afraid their crazy rage *ka-shi* would punch through at any random moment and smash me.

Young was not the only Korean male who had this rage issue. I saw this with many Korean American males. Occasionally, I would see this rage in non-Koreans and females also, but for Korean males, it was passively accepted as the norm. However, excuses like "oh, he's just mad" or "that's just him" prevented many Korean males from confronting and removing their *ka-shis* that unfortunately ended up destroying the relationships in their lives.

Suzi

My friend Suzi and her older sibling lived in an expensive neighborhood with her parents. I admired their family because they seemed to have it together. They were living the American Dream. They had money and expensive furniture, drove imported cars, lived in an expensive gated facility, and were polite. But their "perfect" Korean home was like a fake Hollywood set–a beautiful exterior, but nothing of substance inside. Her family's *ka-shi* was protruding out of her body. It was rotting her.

She and her mom daily faced verbal, emotional, and psychological abuse from the father who left no physical marks on their bodies. She wasn't pretty according to her parent's standards, so her parents compensated with expensive bags, clothes, and other items. Suzi's *ka-shi* began to appear when she secretly took drugs, was negative and down about her appearance, and disappeared after we ate meals together. She was beautiful, but she always thought she was fat and ugly. I watched Suzi suffer for years. It wasn't until later that she admitted to purging, taking multiple diet pills, and desiring to get plastic surgery. Before that, no one suspected she had a problem.

"This is my family. It is what it is. I have money, but I don't have a loving family that accepts, supports, and encourages me for who I am."

"Have you ever talked to someone for help?" I inquired.

"No, I can't. My parents would kill me. I would ruin their reputation. My family is different. A counselor wouldn't understand."

"Well, I wish someone could help you. It's not fair that you have to suffer."

"I know."

"If you know, then you should get some help. It's better to deal with this now before it affects you worse later."

Her face hardened and her mask came up.

"Ahh . . . nevermind. I don't think you understand. It's hard to explain."

Growing up, I began to realize this happened a lot. Children were reminded to *save the family's face* and not embarrass the household. Social reputation for many families seemed more important than the health of young teenagers.

"Be quiet and don't share anything negative about the family."

"Never tell people what goes on inside the home."

"Don't tell people your problems."

"What happens in the house, stays at home."

I felt Suzi's *ka-shi,* and I wished to have taken it out, but I felt powerless and without answers to give her. I wondered how many more of us had hidden *ka-shi*, and if we did, how could we take it out? The *ka-shi* left marks in us that often led to externally harming ourselves. I saw *ka-shi* everywhere, but as soon as they poked through our skin, we covered ourselves with academics, titled positions, status, and money.

We needed help.

Beef It and Beat It

On top of all For typical Korean girls, beauty is based on thinness of body, whiteness of skin, and bigness of eyes. Jenny was not the typical Korean girl. She was tall, possibly 5'7. She was average in weight but overweight by Korean standards, with pale skin but small eyes with no double eyelids.

Jenny hung out with the non-Korean guys and wasn't very popular in the Korean community. In school, the more students there were of a certain ethnicity, the more power those students had. At my school, which was dominated by Koreans, power belonged to us. Korean power. When Jenny hung out with non-Koreans, it demonstrated she did not have the power that other Korean students had.

I don't know what happened, but when Jenny came back from school in her 11th grade year, she came back emaciated—like the K-pop singers. She dressed differently. In the past, she had worn loose jeans and T-shirts, but that year she showed up in tight jeans and a pale green blazer over a white V-neck. Her hair was lightened and cut into a stylish bob, which was shorter in the back with longer strands in the front. In addition, she had put on makeup.

Jenny stopped hanging out with her non-Korean guy friends and spent her time with the older wangstas under the Korean tree. Word around school spread like wildfire. She was now supposedly cool. Losing weight, having a new wardrobe, and changing her face with makeup had an effect on us. We were drawn to her. She became powerful, no longer an overweight nobody, but someone who used her external beauty to gain notoriety and popularity.

I will admit, she looked prettier than before, and it may have been due to her makeup. She used Korean cake powder, the kind you could only find at the Korean supermarket or the small Korean beauty stores in Koreatown. It made her skin flawless.

The transformation of Jenny appealed to me. I wanted to use Korean makeup to enhance my features as well.

"Mom, can I get some makeup?" I asked her one day. "I want

to try the Korean cake powder. A lot of the girls are buying Korean cake powder for their faces."

"You have good skin and you don't need makeup. Why do you ask all of a sudden?"

"No reason."

As months went by, somebody spilled it. Jenny purged. Ken told me that she purged so much that she couldn't eat red meat anymore. Red meat? Like *galbi*? Like *bulgogi*? Who would want to give up *galbi*?

My image of Jenny shattered. She was no longer powerful and awe-inspiring. Instead, she was still the insecure girl who didn't love herself enough. She concentrated on changing her external attributes rather than embracing her true inner beauty. Since I observed her from a distance, I couldn't tell her that internal beauty was more important than her external looks. Even if I had told her she was already beautiful, she wouldn't have believed me because she had already covered up her *ka-shi* with clothes, Korean makeup, and a costly thinness.

On top of that, she couldn't eat Korean *galbi*.

That, to me, was disappointing.

Lee Suh Bin

Allison, or Lee Suh Bin, was different. She looked like a tomboy who didn't play sports. She wore baggy pants and oversized white and occasionally black T-shirts that were bought at the swap meet to cover up her well-endowed breasts, which were not common for Korean females. Her hair was sometimes down or in a ponytail. She was quiet most of the time and kept to herself.

I, too, was a tomboy who didn't look like one but loved to play sports. Sometimes I wore baggy pants and T-shirts, and often put my hair in a ponytail. I was loud and sometimes too hyper and said things I shouldn't have. Other times, I was quiet as a mouse. I loved playing sports and joined the guys whenever they went snowboarding or hiking. I disliked wearing dresses unless it was Homecoming, Winter Formal, or Prom. But I don't think Lee Suh Bin ever went to a formal dance with a guy. I just assumed no one asked her or she didn't know how to dance.

During high school, I would go to her house once in a while. We played video games, shot some hoops, talked, and drew pictures. I just thought she was slightly different, but so was I. Some of my classmates used to make fun of her, but I didn't. If my classmates talked about other people in front of me, I was pretty sure they also talked about me behind my back.

"She's a tomboy," a student often stated.

"So, what's wrong with being a tomboy? I'm one, too," I retorted.

"She's a lesbian," another student chimed in.

"No, she's not. She just likes to wear boy clothes. Leave her alone," I told them.

"Whatever you wanna think." Amy shrugged her shoulders.

Lee Suh Bin was shy and insecure but very introspective, smart, artistic, and nice. She had great potential in becoming an artist, and often sketched images of shoes, people, and other items in her notebook. She was quite talented. However, money, family issues, and her insecurities hindered her from blossoming. These three hidden *ka-shi* occurred in many Korean households.

Some of these issues were more potent while others were less potent. Lee Suh Bin was unable to attend professional art school or additional tutoring programs or *hakwons* because money was tight.

After high school, we all went to different colleges, and I gradually lost contact with a lot of my high school friends. One day though I ran into one of my Korean friends from my old community.

"Did you hear about Lee Suh Bin?" my friend asked.

"No, why? How is she doing?" I wanted to know. "I haven't spoken to her in a long time."

"Well, it's out."

"Huh? Did she go to art school and become famous?" I asked.

"No. She's a lesbian."

"Huh? What? How is that so? Really?"

"Well, she is. She came out."

"How can she? Are there Korean lesbians, especially in our community?" I asked with naiveté. Sometimes I caught myself saying things without thinking.

"Uh, yeah. It doesn't matter if you're Korean or not," she stated flatly.

Shocked, I stood there thinking. Past memories flooded my mind. I recalled our times when we talked about girls who were pretty and ugly, but I didn't think it was abnormal. In fact, most of my girlfriends and I had often analyzed girls in beauty magazines, and we had scrutinized Korean females at our school, similar to how the *ahjummas* analyzed us.

I wondered if other people knew where she was. Most importantly, I wondered if her parents knew her sexual preference. For a Korean to be a lesbian was something that wasn't shared with anyone. We were from a small neighborhood, and in that community, news traveled fast, especially with the *ahjummas*. If the secret came out among our first generation parents, it would be a nightmare; especially for Lee Suh Bin's parents, who attended a big, local church. If the word got out, the chatter would never end. Her parents would be rejected from the Korean community, and her peers and community would blackball Lee Suh Bin. Maybe her "secret" led her to live a quiet life.

Holding onto this secret must have been so difficult for her. I understood. No matter what, she would be stuck. She barely had friends in school because she was rejected for being different. If she came out, she would have no friends. Korean girls would not want to share food with her or give her a hug, thinking she might like them.

I wondered if her sexual preference was the reason I didn't hear from her after high school. Although I don't swing in her direction, I did miss her.

After a couple of weeks, another of my friends asked me, "Did you hear about Lee Suh Bin?"

"No," I said. I didn't like to gossip.

"Well, I heard she's a lesbian."

"Oh, really." I remarked. "Well, try not to spread the news to everyone. I don't think it's your business to share with people."

In our Korean community, no one would have wanted to know if a Korean girl was a closet lesbian. We didn't talk about homosexuality. It was something that didn't exist and no one talked about it if it did. The hope was that as long as Koreans did not open Pandora's box, maybe people would not know we had any problems. From many adults' perspectives, it was best to leave the *ka-shi* inside of people rather than prying it out. I wasn't sure if people knew that the life we lived hurt us, especially Lee Suh Bin.

Gi Shin

Gi Shin was a dutiful first-born daughter who was obedient, well-mannered in front of adults, and studious. She had nothing but positive and good characteristics as a child. She spoke Korean and English well. When asked to help prepare food, clean the house, and take care of her siblings, she cheerfully helped her mother and father.

However, I had not known the nice Gi Shin. To me, she was more like the devil's child. She tormented me on a daily basis when I was in high school; a vampire that sucked the life out of me, beat my soul down, and injected my body with *ka-shi*.

I was not sure why I was her victim. I minded my own business and did what was good. I was the bubbly, funny Sarai, except when she was around.

"So, you think you're so good, Sarai?" she sneered at me. She frequently taunted me, and at other times, she pointed out things about me to make me feel insecure. "You dumb shit. You're trying to live life like a good girl. You'll end up miserable and lonely."

Fear, anger, pain, and despair pierced my insides when she bullied me. I wondered if it was due to my short stature, skinny but athletic body, or what. I was just a bystander who became a victim for no apparent reason, a breathing human being who happened to be in her class.

In the beginning, I kept my mouth shut. Sometimes I kept quiet and took in her fire-breathing curses; other times, I walked away so she wouldn't see me crying. Scared out of my wits, there were times when I wanted to stand up for myself. I had to. My classmates and friends didn't do anything; they remained silent bystanders. But I was Sarai, someone who was happy and funny and got along with everyone. I didn't want to be sad and miserable. Unfortunately, I had a difficult time standing up for myself. My voice quivered and my body shivered.

"Buh, buh, buh, why do you stutter, Bitch?"

Gi Shin was bold and wasn't scared of anyone, especially not me. She used her words to stab people. Her haughty diatribes and foul language would lodge in my soul and rot my belly. I was in turmoil. Just thinking about Gi Shin made me become another person. Anger, rage, and hate stirred inside of me. I didn't want these feelings, but her demons penetrated through my skin and made me act the same way.

"If you have something to say, say it!" she jabbed me with her shoulder.

I was timid, but I think she wanted me to stand up for myself.

"Come on. You have anything to say to me, then say it! Shit."

I wondered if she wanted me to learn how to fight for myself. I couldn't.

Years passed. Although I tried to forget Gi Shin, seeing her spectre saunter down the school halls brought shivers down my spine.

I had to say something, or I would become rotting dry bones.

"What do you want? You have something to say to me?" she taunted.

"I want you to stop bothering me!" I yelled one day.

"What's your problem, Bitch?"

"You. You're my problem. Stop tormenting me. Leave me alone!" I was shaking with fear because her face was a few inches from mine. She was really good at intimidating me. But it was time to fight back. "For many years, you've bullied me. You've made fun of me. You've made me miserable. Just STOP!" I pulled back the tears, but my voice still quivered uncontrollably.

"Well, this is the first time you stood up." She took a step back, surprised. "Not too bad. You're lucky we know similar people because if we didn't, I'd smash your face and kick the shit out of you."

"Just stop it! Leave me alone! You can have my friends. Just stop it!" I walked away from her.

I was 17. It took many years to muster the courage to open my mouth. I wanted to be the quiet leader who didn't have to open my mouth, but keeping quiet would continue the torment. Teachers and counselors would be of no help. They were too busy to see what was happening behind the scenes with the students. Unless something big happened, they would not step in.

During the time of my tormenting days, I couldn't understand who she was and why she was so evil. However, from classmates and friends' responses, I began making connections.

She grew up in a Christian home, and they all went to church. Her mother was very devout and wailed during midnight hours, and her father was a workaholic that provided for the family so they could live and eat. People said that something happened to her when she moved to our quiet suburban community. Whether it was her pubescent years, the move, a new school, or something more sinister, the root issue was not found.

She began smoking around 14 years of age. She spent time with older people who became her friends and began dating older men. Whether or not she was promiscuous was of question, but many people said she was available. In addition, marijuana, speed, and possibly coke were some of the drugs she experimented. Next came piercings and forbidden tattoos, alongside an all-black wardrobe. She was dark.

Her mother wailed for her daughter to come back to the Lord, but I think Gi Shin sold herself to the devil. She wasn't normal. The times she tormented me, it seemed like spirits possessed her. Even more strangely, she didn't torment other people to this extent. There were times when she snapped at and criticized others when she didn't like them or thought they were dumb, but it was never to the extent of how she plagued me.

When adults wanted to correct her behavior and attitude, she made condescending remarks. Wherever she went, she experienced devaluing words, negative criticisms, and glaring stares from Koreans. Though she was devilish, her behavior may have been a reaction to her internal struggle with too many *ka-shi*. She was a depressed and oppressed soul, and the only way to make her life worth living was to poke herself with needles as well as puncture other people's souls. These negative *ka-shi* infused her and infected people wherever she went. Although I stood up to her, Gi Shin's *ka-shi* deeply gouged my soul.

There's Still More

Jenna was the top of her class. She was a busy bee who didn't seem to stop nor take a break. At school, her lunch periods were filled with daily clubs meetings that she and her high-achieving friends led. In school, she took advanced placement courses and was in leadership positions; she participated in multiple community service and leadership programs outside of school and went to *hakwons*, Korean run academy schools, to increase her SAT, ACT, SAT II, and Advanced Placement scores on her official exams.

During the summer, she participated in academic programs at various prestigious liberal arts colleges and took extra courses at a local community college. When she was in 11th grade, she began working at various community organizations where she had previously volunteered when she was in middle school. To top it off, she was a finalist for the National Honors Society and won a few regional awards. She was an elite, polished and packaged to position herself for her college career.

I became her afterschool friend at the local *hakwon* we went to. I admired her ability to do everything while maintaining A's in all her classes. She was assertive and bossy. She was nice to me possibly because I cracked jokes in class and was nice to her when others didn't like her.

"How do you do everything? You're so busy." I asked her one day when she took some time to drink her diet coke during break at the *hakwon*. It was the summer of our junior year, and she was already completing her college applications. I had yet to start on mine.

"Well, when you have a goal in mind, then you do whatever it takes to get there," she responded.

"Where do you want to go?" I inquired. Her eyes focused and pierced into my eyes as if she was telling me to get serious about my college career.

"I want to go to one of the top institutions in the United States."

"Why top?" I inquired.

85

"I've prepared my entire life to get accepted to the top 10 prestigious colleges and universities." She was trying to be modest, but there was a sense of pride and false humility that seeped out of her mouth. I could see why people didn't like her. Her prideful undertone and emotionless facial features intimidated other students. I didn't mind.

"Is there a particular college you want to attend? If you prepared your entire life for the top 10, then wouldn't you have one specific college you really want to go to." I hadn't figured out my college list. I had hoped speaking to ambitious Jenna would help me to figure out where I would go.

"Just the top 10. I prefer Harvard, but I'm going to keep my options open. Stanford is my next choice."

With more than 3,000 colleges and universities, I wondered if she kept her options open. For me, there were too many colleges to choose from, and when my school counselor said to pick 8-10 colleges, limiting my college choices seemed overwhelming.

"If you're so focused and want to apply to the top 10 colleges, do you plan to apply to all of them?" Not only did she have to apply to colleges, but she also had to pay for the application, registration, and, eventually, housing and tuition. A college diploma was one of the most expensive pieces of paper that I knew of.

"Of course! The statistics of these colleges accepting Asians are limited because of the class size. Plus, some colleges think we are the model minorities which may make it difficult for us to be admitted."

"I didn't know that. I thought if a person did well, then they would get into a particular college."

Shaking her head, she gave me a condescending look. "Did you not know that people who get accepted to these top colleges have been groomed and prepared? You have to be the best, well-rounded, and excel in something that is beyond a leadership position at school. Some may see it as luck, but it isn't. It's a game, and there's competition out there, and I want to do whatever it takes to make it to the top. In particular, we Asians—no, Koreans—have a more difficult task when it comes to the college process. College admission representatives may think we are innately smart, but they don't know how much work it takes. To top it off, there's about 4% of the Asian population in the nation and people and universities think there's too many of us at their colleges."

Jenna's body tensed and she was breathing heavily. She took a few deep breaths to calm her heart and then took a few sips of her diet coke. Refocusing on centering herself, she turned and smiled at me. I wondered if the other high achieving Asian students knew what she was talking about. I was grateful for her information and wondered if she shared her thoughts with other students.

Nah. I think she freely shared with me because she knew I wasn't part of her competition. Barely hitting average scores on my college entrance exams, I was just a middle-of-the-road Korean American who needed help with academics and with concentrating. My parents said I was too energized for a Korean female, and they thought that sending me to *hakwon* would help me improve my grades and wear out my energy by the time I came home.

After processing what she stated, I inquired, "Jenna, why do you think of the college process as competition?"

"I must get to the top college. It's my life!" She exclaimed.

"College is only one step; there's still more to life than college," I said.

She shook her head. "You got it wrong. My parents sacrificed their lives so that I would get into a prestigious college, and hopefully, a full ride. Look at the sacrifice your parents made to send you to *hakwon*. I'm pretty sure your parents want the best for you."

"I guess so," I murmured. My parents wanted me to do well and go to a good college. With thousands of colleges to go to, I believed almost all of them were good.

"Think about it, Sarai. You only have one life. Wouldn't you want to go to the best school and make something of yourself?"

"Yes, of course. But I also think we need to discover who we are and what we are supposed to do in life. I see success as more than attending a brand name college." Honestly, I didn't care about a brand name college, but many people around me did.

87

"Exactly. I figured it out. I'm going to get accepted to the top universities and become successful in life."

Admiring her intense tenacity, perseverance, and drive to be excellent, I smiled.

During her senior year, with a lack of sleep, too many responsibilities to handle, college applications to complete, and college essays to write, Jenna cracked. The pressure was too much.

Entering into the bathroom at the *hakwon*, I quickly saw Jenna wipe her tears.

"Are you okay?" I asked.

"Yea . . ." She pretended to be okay. She wasn't.

"Well, I'm here if you need to talk. I'm available." About to lock the bathroom stall, I peered to my right and saw the tears stream down her cheeks. Her eyeliner was smearing and I could hear the wad of snot in her nose.

"I'm okay."

"Okay . . ."

"It's just so much! I've been doing all of this and I don't think I'll make it. I don't think I've done enough!" She gasped for air and then blew her snot.

"Uh-huh." I came out of the stall and headed towards her to comfort her. At this time, snot came out of her nose and found its way into her mouth. I was thinking about hugging her, but it was too gross.

"You'll be fine. You've prepared all your life for this. You'll get to college. Don't worry." I tried to pay attention to her concern and words, but it was a struggle to focus on her internal issues instead of her outer mess.

"But it won't be the top 10! You don't understand!"

"Well, you kind of limited yourself. Ten colleges? I have about 3,000, and I'm having a hard time choosing which college to go to."

"You don't understand."

Choking up, her head bobbled up and down. Between her and me, she didn't understand.

"By the way," I said, "are you sleeping?"

"What do you mean?"

"You look a bit exhausted." Whether it was her eye-liner or

SEOUL FOOD

dark circles, I didn't know.

"Of course I sleep!" she sounded a little offended. "I sleep between periods and when my mom is driving me to my next activity." She compromised her sleeping schedule with a rigorous course load and activities.

Besides her snot and smeared eye-liner, her breath was ferocious. Maybe I was too close to her, but her breath was worse than my *kimchi*-garlic breath. Usually, one of the signs of bad breath was hunger. She probably was depleted of energy with all the work she was doing, and she may have not eaten a lot. Besides her diet coke, I rarely saw her eat.

"Did you eat?" I asked. "When is the last time you ate?"

"Yes, I already ate," she snapped at me. "I eat when I have time." The crying stopped and she looked away from me. "I eat. Okay?" Her response sounded a bit defensive.

This could only mean one thing. She knew that her eating issues had been discovered. During high school, many people were concerned with their weight, height, skin color, and appearance. Jenna, not having a lot of friends, was smart, not too skinny, not so pretty, and not popular.

"Why do you ask?" She wiped her tears with a paper towel.

"Well, I only see you drinking diet coke a lot. I've never seen you eat food at the *hakwon* or at school. You know, I roam on campus here and there. I see you, but I don't really see you eat food."

"I'm not hungry." She retorted. "I'm fine. Thanks for listening. I would like to be left alone now." She briskly went into the bathroom stall and locked herself. "You can go, I'm fine!"

That was rude. Here I was trying to comfort her while she looked like a total mess inside and outside. I just got pushed aside. Tilting my head towards the closed bathroom stall, I peeked through the open crack to see her. At that moment, I realized what the other students meant when they said she was curt and selfish. She only talked to me when she felt like it, and shut me off when she didn't. Since I couldn't convince her to see her situations from a different perspective, I left the bathroom.

Despite the fact that she appeared put together and well off, the incident was the first time she cried and let her guard down in public. That day, her *ka-shi* overflowed. She had hidden her pain,

89

struggles, and pressures to try to become "perfect," but the pressure of college applications may have been the last *ka-shi* that broke her.

At that time, I wondered what kind of life she lived at home and what kind of relationship she had with her parents. Reflecting on my previous conversations with her, I could safely assume her family struggled with finances because she said her parents sacrificed a lot for her and desired for her to get a college scholarship. I wasn't college savvy, but I knew poorer students would be able to get financial aid.

At school and *hakwon,* her personality and behavior changed. It was difficult to determine when she would be nice to people or bite their heads off. I avoided her during our senior year because I didn't want her to snap at me, and because Gi Shin was already tormenting me.

In second semester of our senior year, I came to find out that she was accepted to one of the top 10 colleges in the nation. She chose a liberal arts college over a public university and received a lot of scholarship money for her accomplishments. It came to my attention that she was malnourished, and that her lack of sleep affected her during her first year in college. She was simply burned out.

This was something I didn't want to do or become. When I looked at Jenna, I learned the most important thing was to take care of myself—eat, sleep, and be balanced. At the end of the day, what was so important about attending a prestigious university? Would the college give her happiness and peace? I doubted it.

Blepharoplasty

I grew up hearing we needed to love ourselves for who we are. However, being Korean in America was somewhat difficult when our outer beauty was perceived to be of higher importance than our inner beauty–especially for females.

"Is your face small?"

"Do you have good skin?"

"Do you have light skin?"

"Do you look and act feminine?"

"And, do you have double eyelids? Yes, double eyelids!"

Double eyelids were a physical trait that was, had been, and still is the craze for many Korean females. Having double eyelids was something to possess. Koreans who were born with them would often hear compliments like, "Oh, your eyes are so pretty," or "Oh, your eyes are so big!" Other times, older parents would comment, "She would look pretty if she got eye surgery."

Most likely, those with the double eyelids did in fact have surgery; parents would pay for their daughters and occasionally for their sons to get eyelid surgery. A handful of girls in Korea received plastic surgery as their high school graduation present, and the same happened here in my LA community. Many would fly to Seoul over the summer or winter to get their eyes done. Often, we could tell if people had surgery. A few lucky ones got them naturally. The rest, those who wanted double eyelids but couldn't afford surgery, used tape or glue to form them.

My mom was in the lucky category. She had natural double eyelids. My dad didn't, but it was okay because he was a male.

"Mom, will I get double eyelids like you?" I asked her often.

"You will get it when you are in your twenties," she would tell me every time I asked her. I think I asked her at least twice a month from the time I was young.

"Mom, why are your eyes so big?" I asked.

"Big to see you," she chuckled. "I get to see everything you do, so be careful."

"Mom, how come your double eyelids are perfect?" I commented.

"It's because of you. You gave me too much stress."

She explained child rearing in America was very difficult. Being a stay-at-home mother in America, whose husband constantly worked while she took care of three rambunctious children, who were extremely different from each other, took a toll on her.

"I was tired and stressed. The lines started coming in deeper. And, as I got older, my eyes started to droop. That's why I have double eyelids." Was this true?

I was never good at waiting, and I didn't want to let nature take its course. No, I had to do something about it. For about a week, I purposely stressed myself out by wasting time and staying up all night. But instead of getting a line, my eyes just got puffy. They shrank in size. So, that didn't work.

I then decided to find out from classmates how they had double eyelids. I knew some girls who put tape or glue above their eyes, and then tried to pretend it was natural, which everyone knew it wasn't. These girls opened their eyes really wide and didn't blink when people spoke to them. This just made them look scary. When they stared at me with their unblinking eyes, I ended up with a scared and surprised look myself. I couldn't help it--I sometimes unconsciously mimicked whoever I was speaking with. Some of the girls would look away. When they looked away, I would look at where they were staring.

"What are you looking at?" I often asked.

"Nothing."

They were busy trying to not stare at you because they didn't want you to know they had tape or glue on their eyes. "Do you think people won't know if you look away?" I thought to myself.

Other girls put a lot of eyeliner and eyeshadow over the tape or crease area. When they looked down or closed their eyes, all I saw was black all around their eyes. They reminded me of Elvira.

Some Korean females opted for glue instead of tape to get the double eyelid effect. Sometimes, the white glue would clump. It would dry up and leave white lines above their eyes. Some used super strength strong glue that set the lines so deep into the eye socket that when they opened their eyes to reveal their double eyelids, they couldn't close them again. Imagine having a hard time blinking. I wondered if they put eye drops to moisten their eyes.

During class, some girls would whisper to each other, "Can you see it?" Friends would say "no" even though it was apparent that their eyes looked unnatural. Others would turn their back on the teacher, bend over, and put some glue over their eyes to have double eyelids in class.

"What are you doing Jenny"? Ms. Lee asked. She was the Korean teacher at our school.

Bending down, Jenny said, "Nothing. I'm just checking to see if there's something in my eyes." The other girls who were her friends covered for her. It was a silent secret to not have people know the girls used glue and tape. But, it definitely was not a secret.

I was determined. I was young, and I couldn't wait another 10 years for my double eyelids. At home, I got scotch tape and cut it into strips. I put the tape on top of my eye. There was no fold. I then pulled the tape off. It hurt. I tried again. My eyes folded on one side but the other side looked as if I had slanted eyes. I pulled off the tape. It hurt again. My skin became a little pink. I cut new pieces of tape and tried again. The fold was too big, and I looked like an alien. After spending some time trying to make the tape work, I decided that I needed to ask the "experts" at my school.

The experts were a selected few who were really good at gluing. The way they put their glue on was so perfect that it was impossible to see the glue when they blinked. It may have been because they were a pro or their eyes stretched so much that there was enough skin to be embedded in their eye socket.

"What are you talking about?" said Jane.

At first, she denied she did anything with her eyes. But I explained to her that I knew she used glue, and I told her she had the best fake double eyelids.

"Please, teach me how to do my eyes. My mom said I would get double eyelids naturally in my twenties, but I can't wait."

After begging her for some time, she finally gave in. Jane suggested I go to the Korean market.

"Don't go to the American markets. They won't know what you are talking about. They don't know what double eyelids are. When you go, go to the front counter where they sell makeup and lotions. Ask the *ahjumma* for some eye tape and fake eyelashes. There, the lady will give you a strip of precut tape that's shaped like half moons. Also, consider buying Korean or Japanese fake eyelashes."

"Wow! I didn't know there's precut eye tape!"

"The fake eyelashes come with glue. There are two types of glue. One has a white top and the other has a yellow top. The white one is weaker than the yellow one. I use the white one, but because you are new, try the white one at home and then the yellow one when you go out. After, make sure you wash your eyes with soap and warm water. Don't just pull off the glue or tape because it'll stretch your lids and then you'll have sagging eyes. After that, you'll definitely need eye surgery."

"Oh, really! I didn't know that. I tried putting tape on my eyes and when I took it off, it was pink. It hurt."

She peered at me as if I should've known.

The next time my mom wanted to go to the Korean market, I quickly volunteered to help her. She went to the *banchan* aisle, and I went towards the makeup counter and bought both tape and glue. The tape strip had about 10 precut pairs. I looked at the tape and realized it was medical tape. I had this at home. Why didn't I think about using medical tape?

I went home and headed straight to the bathroom, washed my face, and then put the tape above my eyes.

Wow! My eyes looked very big. I blinked and opened my eyes.

I came out of the bathroom and went to Janice.

"How do I look?"

"Scary," she said. "Stop trying to be like the other girls. Your eyes are big and you don't need it."

"But, how do my eyes look? Don't they look big?" I asked with glee.

"Scary," she firmly restated.

I went to Frank and asked him. I thought my brother would be more supportive.

"How do my eyes look?"

"What?" He responded.

"My eyes. Don't you see the fold?" I said.

"Whatever. You already have big eyes."

Siblings were not helpful. I took off the tape. That hurt. I think my skin stretched when I peeled the tape; I forgot to wash it off.

The next day, Jane asked me what happened.

"My eyes looked really big, but my sister said I looked scary."

"Yes. That can happen. You have to find a natural line so you don't look like a monster."

"How do you put the tape on to make it look natural?" I inquired.

"Well, there are some steps you have to do. Some people may do it differently, but I like to do it with these steps."

"What are the steps?" I asked with excitement. I didn't know there were steps I needed to take.

"When I wake up in the morning, I wash my face, brush my teeth, you know, the morning stuff. I dry my face, but I don't use any toner or lotion. My eyes have to be dry."

I leaned forward, listening intently.

"I take the tape out of the package, but I don't use my fingers. I don't want the adhesive to wear off. I get tweezers or a small stick. Now, at this point, I know where the tape goes. After some practice, you'll know where the tape should go. I visualize the spot and place the tape there. Then I use tweezers and push my lid deep into my eye socket where the top tape line is. Some people use a toothpick or a specially made tape fork. I'm ghetto and don't want to purchase a special fork. My tweezers are good enough."

"If I don't like the way my eye looks, I start over again. I make sure to wash off with warm water and soap. Don't be like the other girls who don't care if they'll have droopy eyes in the future. You need to wash your face and gently take the tape off. Anyway, once I have my eye shape, I put eyeliner on top of the tape."

"Wow! I didn't know there were certain ways to put tape on my eyes. What about glue?" I asked.

"Glue is slightly different, and it takes practice. It's about right timing, or the glue will be too wet or too dry. You need to practice."

"Okay, I'll practice. But, can you tell me how you do it?"

"Well, I only use tape because I prefer using it over glue. However, I've tried glue before. Some people get special eye glue, but like I said, you can use the glue that comes with the fake eyelashes. Put the glue on where you would like the crease to be. Try putting the glue closer towards your eyes because you have virgin eyes. Once you make a line, wait for about 20-45 seconds for the glue to settle in. Get the tweezers or a bobby pin and push your eyes into your eye socket. Make sure to press in the area and wait for about 30 seconds to one minute. Don't let go of your spot and press again, or you'll make the glue clump and your eyes might not stay. If you don't like how it looks, try again. If you do, then you can put on eyeshadow and eyeliner."

"Wow, thanks!"

"One warning. Your eyes may stretch. You may look good now, but you'll have droopy eyes earlier than later."

Although I received the warning, I still needed to try. Droopy or not, I wanted double eyelids. It was now or maybe later. I opted for now.

After school, I went home. I washed my face and then tried the glue. The glue was a strong adhesive because it was made to hold fake eyelashes right above real lashes. Using glue was difficult. The first time, the glue clumped. The second time, the glue was too dry. After trying multiple times, I got it right. The glue set in and I had a fold. I was ready to show my sister.

"How do I look?" I asked Janice.

"Scary," she remarked. "You have white stuff showing and it looks really messy."

I looked at myself in the mirror. The once great line was flaky and white. My double eyelid didn't set in.

Time wasted.

I continued to practice at home, but as time progressed, I got tired of putting on tape and glue. My mom had said I would get my double eyelids naturally in my twenties. I decided to believer her. I decided to wait and learn patience.

Mama's Boy

Our parents didn't really know their children. When we came home from school, they did not ask how we were doing or if there was anything going on with our lives. They wanted to know about grades, school, test scores, and getting ready to go to college. Some of us responded to the pressure by getting really poor grades. Others did whatever it took to please their parents.

Amy cheated on her exams to get A's. The pressure she felt at home was to be the best. Cheating helped her to get into a prestigious college and then to med school, but she eventually dropped out.

Sarah was not smart like her brother, so she worked doubly hard. She was very alert in her classes, and at home, she studied past midnight. Her parents must have been proud of her when she stayed up all night to study. She was a great example of a diligent daughter with a vibrant but jittery personality. Unfortunately, Sarah was also addicted to speed.

Paul did his best to hide his issues by smoking, taking ecstasy, and drinking alcohol. He was one of the bad boys in school and got into trouble, especially with his teachers and people who ticked him off. Fights and angry outbursts were common for him but for some strange reason, he had decent grades.

My mom often told me to stay away from people who were not good influences. Since Paul had a bad reputation, I only observed his behavior from afar. I couldn't understand why he would make bad decisions that could affect his college career. It was not until later when I saw how much pain, stress, and sadness he carried that I knew. His dad was physically, verbally, and emotionally abusive to him, using fear, manipulation, and control to scare Paul. At home, Paul was the submissive son, but outside, he was like his father. *Ka-shis* were deeply embedded in his body.

At the end of the day, school was only a part of our lives, but our souls would remain with us. We needed an outlet, a way to communicate to our parents regarding how we thought and felt. We needed our souls to be healed.

Then again, some parents may have overlooked us while others over-protected us. I will never forget Stephen and his relationship with his mom.

Stephen's mother was a stay-at-home mom with an unhappy marriage. She made sure Stephen had food on his plate, that his clothes were clean, and his needs were met. His mother picked him up from school, dropped him at tutoring centers, and took him around wherever he needed to go. At night when he studied, his mother brought him drinks and fruit to eat. His mother had served his needs since he was born and hadn't stopped. Her child was her life.

When Stephen reached his mid-twenties, he had a part-time job and still lived at home. On weekends, he would take his mother to the market and shopping centers so she could get some fresh air. Stephen was definitely a momma's boy, but he didn't think of himself that way. He just believed his mother loved him.

"Why would I get my own apartment when my mom takes care of me," he shared with me. "When I get married, I will leave or my wife will live with my family. My mom suffered so much. I want to take care of her before she dies. It's better to take care of her now than later."

Stephen then met a young woman, Inhae. He was happy to have a girlfriend. He began to spend his weekends more and more with Inhae and less with his mother.

"I don't like her," his mother said without ever meeting her.

"She's nice. You'll like her."

"Well, I don't. But, I want to see her. I want to see this fox."

When she did finally see Inhae, she said, "She's ugly and fat."

"Well, she was a model, and she's not fat. She's skinnier than you."

"Don't say that to me."

"Sorry, Mom."

"Well, I don't like her, and she's going to be trouble."

The trouble was with the mother. Stephen had to constantly be sure he spent enough time with his mother and girlfriend.

"You will have to win her over," Stephen told Inhae. So, the first time she went over to Stephen's place, she brought the mother gifts of plants, food, and pastries as a polite gesture. Gifts and thank you's were exchanged, but it wasn't good enough.

"My mom says you are a fox," he said to his girlfriend the next day.

"Why are you letting me know?" Inhae wondered.

"Well, I just want you to be nice to my mom. She may be a little overbearing, but she does it out of love. You'll get used to her and you will like her, too."

The next time Inhae came to his house, she bowed and said hello.

Ignoring Inhae, Stephen's mother asked him, "Did you eat Stephen?"

"I'm not hungry, but I think Inhae is hungry. Did you eat?" he asked Inhae.

"No, but it's okay," she replied. "I'm not that hungry."

"Well, let's get some food when we go out."

"Why do you eat out when you don't have money?" Stephen's mother interjected. "I'll make you something because you don't have money."

On multiple occasions, when Inhae and Stephen had made plans together, his mother would think of reasons to keep him at home. Inhae tried many ways to please Stephen's mother, but it didn't matter what she did. She recognized that Stephen's mother wanted her out of the picture.

One day Inhae broached the subject with Stephen. "Your mother seems attached to you."

"My mom loves me and shows me how much she cares for me. She cooks, cleans the house, and cleans my clothes."

"Does she clean your underwear?"

"Yes, that's a stupid question. My dirty clothes go in the hamper and she washes it. She even loves me so much that she hand washes it."

"This is not normal. This is gross."

"It's not gross. In the olden days, they hand-washed their clothes."

"Yes, but we have washers and dryers."

"When a mother loves his son, she would do anything for him. My mom loves me and I love my mom."

Inhae really liked Stephen, but soon realized his future wife would have to cook, clean, do the laundry, take care of his needs, and do all the housework. The relationship ended sourly.

"I told you she was a fox," his mother said. "Next time, listen to me when I tell you I don't like someone."

"*Neh*." Stephen nodded and hugged his mother.

PART 3

JEON

Jeon is a pancake-like dish made from a variety of vegeta-bles, meats, and seafood.

Jeon

Some people are like the chewy pancakes called *buchimgae* or *jeon*. Whereas my American friends ate chocolate chip pancakes, blueberry pancakes, potato pancakes, and plain pancakes, my Mom fed us savory *jeon* with green onions, bits of squid, mushroom, carrots, and other veggies.

She would first slice the carrots, squid, and green onions into thin strips. Then she would get some sort of Korean pancake mix, pour out the powder, and combine it with egg and water. It looked like pancake mix, and every time I saw that mix, I thought mom would make American-style fluffy pancakes; but then she would gently stir in mixed veggies. Next, she would put a flat pan on the stove and turn the heat to medium high. Rather short, I would bring a chair to the kitchen and sit up on the counter. Usually, little Korean children shouldn't sit on the counter. I was glad mom was different and didn't mind.

Mom would then drizzle some oil on the pan and turn the heat to medium. Taking a scoopful of the liquid mixed veggies, she would nicely pour the mix onto the pan in the shape of a circle. I could hear the sizzle and smell the delicious pancake mix. I was always the first person to taste it.

"Isn't this delicious?" Mom would ask.

"It's so much better than American pancakes. Who would have thought that using vegetables instead of fruits could taste so hearty and good?" American pancakes were bland and not as healthy as Korean pancakes. Whenever I ate mom's *buchimgae,* I would feel strong. Mom made Korean pancakes at least once a month, and no matter what combination of vegetables were in the *jeon,* it was delicious.

"Have you noticed the different types of vegetables I use to make the *jeon*?" She inquired one day.

"Yeah, I notice the different vegetable combinations. You want me to eat a variety of vegetables so I can grow."

"Yes, but I want you to know that no matter what food pieces you combine, the *jeon* will always be good as long as you prevent it from burning."

"Okay." I dipped the chewy pancake in soy sauce and took a big bite.

"Life can be like *jeon,* Sarai."

"Life is about *jeon.* So yummy."

"Wherever you go, you will have various encounters and will come to experience what to do and what not to do, how to live and how not to live. The choices people make lead them to various paths. My hope for you is that you will mature from your experiences and never become charred in life. Observe people because if you don't pay attention, you will be burned by people and in life. I want you to always be a flavorful *jeon* who will spice up the lives around you."

Jeon is a smooth liquid blend that forms into new shapes and creates different tastes when combined with different ingredients. Mom wanted to teach me that I was like *jeon,* a delectable blend of the various people and events that shaped my identity.

Choose Your Nah-moo!

"Nah-moo!!!" Mom said with anger.

"Why do I need to find some wood? I'm only six years old, mommy."

Mom was mad. Occasionally, my parents would get angry and upset at my siblings and me for some reason or another. Pleading for mercy was my first line of defense, but it often backfired because we were disobedient, bad children.

I sincerely wanted to stay on their good side, but besides being quiet and sitting still when they told me to, I didn't know what good really meant. Just like any child, I was a little energized, and a little undomesticated. Climbing trees and running all over the place were ways to expend my energy.

On television shows, like *Family Matters* and *Full House*, I saw adults talk to their children. They discussed their disagreements and resolved their conflicts. Young children or teenagers might have yelled and cried, but they weren't physically punished. At home, weapons such as branches, clothing accessories, bare hands, or anything my parents could grasp in the heat of their raging moments, were used to teach us a lesson.

During these vehement moments, I despised my parents for being Korean, and I despised being born to parents who punished me in this manner. I wondered if they were the only Korean adults who physically punished us for not obeying them. Then I would remember hearing about child abuse cases and realize that this wasn't just my problem. Many children were victims of our parents' lack of patience. It wasn't our fault they couldn't control their own emotions or raise us in a loving manner without using iron fists and fiery mouths.

My siblings and I brought three flimsy sticks to mom.

"Thicker!" Mom yelled.

In fear, we hurriedly went to the backyard, found a few branches from the persimmon and lemon trees, and brought them to her. Mom took off the tiny branches that were protruding from the main branches. She then hit the nude-colored carpet floor to test which weapon would best suit her.

Devising a strategy to avoid the pain, I ran into my room and wore three pants on top of the pants I was already wearing and practiced fake crying. To prevent her from noticing my brilliant plan, I came back looking scared.

"Get up," my mom told all of us. "Turn around." Our backs faced our mom while she got ready.

"Mommy, this is America. You can't abuse us," Janice said.

"That's right. No hitting. It hurts, and we are in America," I chimed in.

"Stop talking," she said. "I'm your mom. And all of you are going to get hit for being disobedient." I still couldn't figure out why we were disobedient. We were a little loud at the restaurant and fidgety in the car.

Janice went first. She tensed her body for the inevitable.

Whack! Whack! Whack! My sister whimpered, and I felt the sting on her butt.

I was next. It was show time.

Thmp. Pause. I began to whimper.

Thmp. I began to cry.

Thmp. Another pause. Silence.

As I cried like my six-year-old self, my mom pulled my pants down, discovering my cushioned layers.

"I knew something was off," she chuckled, her anger quickly subsiding.

Lightening up the mood, I laughed, sat next to my mom, and quickly pushed the sticks underneath the bed to prevent her from hitting us again. Mom didn't notice what I had done. She laughed with all of us, and the spanking stopped.

"Who thought of wearing many pants?" My mom chuckled.

"Well, the *nah-moo* hurts, and I didn't like getting *meh-meh*. I thought wearing pants would help me. Don't be mad. We're all sorry for disobeying you."

"Do you know why you disobeyed?"

"Because we didn't listen to you?"

"And what else?"

"Uh, we were loud?"

"Right. When I tell you to be quiet, you need to be silent. You do this again, you're going to get a *meh-meh*."

"Yes, mommy," I said in response.

"*Neh*," answered Janice and Frank.

I smiled at my mom trying to create a happy mood. She wanted to look upset and angry, but she couldn't hold back the laughter. She shook her head side-to-side, got up, and left to get ready for dinner.

Janice and I looked at each other and giggled.

Although the undeserving punishment era did not stop with this event, I used clever strategies like running away from my parents around the kitchen table, hiding underneath my desk, staying under my bed for the night, and kneeling on my knees to apologize for my sins. Sometimes it worked, and other times, I couldn't escape their wrath.

As a young girl, I couldn't wait to grow up, so I wouldn't be punished in this manner. I thought to myself, "If I were to become a parent, I wouldn't hit my child." Since I knew how my butt and hands felt after a good whack, I wouldn't want my child to go through this pain. I think my parents forgot they were once children who didn't like to be yelled at and hit.

Drug Lord

"Use your words wisely," my mom would remind me. "What you say has so much power."

I understood the significance of the power of words, but I didn't understand why she used to remind me of this more often than she would with my siblings. I decided to find out.

"Mom, why do you only tell *me* to watch what I say?" I asked.

"Because you are very powerful."

"Why me and not Janice and Frank?"

"You're different."

"How am I different, Mom?"

"Because you are dangerous."

"I'm dangerous? I'm different? Mom, I'm your daughter."

"Yes, but when you speak, power comes out."

Great. When I spoke with my mouth, there was a lot of power that came out of me. Did she mean burps? I burped a lot, but this was only to digest my food. I guess it was powerful because my burps were potent, loud, and obnoxious.

"Mom, I don't understand. Can you let me know why you think I have power? Is it because of my burps?"

"No, don't you remember?"

"Remember, what?"

"*Aigoo.*" She shook her head as if I should have remembered.

"You were around four years old, and I took you and Frank to a preschool. Well, we took you to many preschools. Do you ever wonder why you went to many preschools?"

"To get a lot of exposure," I said.

"You moved around because you were the dangerous one. At this one preschool, I came to pick you up and found you sitting by yourself crying. I thought something bad happened to you. I then asked the teacher what happened and she told me you did something bad. You drugged everyone. You told the other children, including Frank, that you had candy. You gave them candy as long as you got to ride the tricycle."

I stood there, the memory suddenly flashing in my mind.

The night before I went to preschool that day, I had been sitting on the counter and saw my mom take a couple of blue pills. I asked her if it was candy, and I thought she said yes. I asked her for some, but she wouldn't give me any. After taking the pills, she placed the bottle on the top cupboard so no one could access it. However, I was the year of the monkey, so I often climbed walls, trees, and cabinets. I was the cupboard climber. That night when no one was in the kitchen, I climbed the cupboard and got the bottle. Candy! I have access to candy! I poured out a handful of the blue candy and put it in my pocket.

The next day, I directed my preschool friends to sit in a circle. I told them I had candy and the only way they would get it was to allow me to ride the tricycle. They all agreed to let me use it all day. I handed the candy to each one of my friends and to Frank. I didn't eat the candy myself because I was going to exchange the rest for another activity that I might be interested in, like playing with the best toys in the sandbox.

At first, the blue candy tasted good. The children were smiling as they sucked on the slightly sugary blue coating. But in a couple of minutes, they began frowning, then groaning, then holding their stomachs. Then June, a chubby little girl who liked to eat, threw up. All the children had blue mouths and were sick. One child went to Miss Cindy and complained that she didn't feel good.

In the meantime, I was the only one playing in the yard. Miss Cindy called me to her, and I rode the tricycle as close to her as possible. She bent down and asked me if I gave drugs to the girl. I didn't know what drugs were, so I said no. Miss Cindy asked me again, this time holding onto my forearm.

"Did you give something to her?" the teacher questioned as she pointed to the girl. Her hand still gripped my arm.

"I gave her candy," I said.

"That's not candy. It's medicine! It's drugs! You had all of the children take the medicine except for yourself."

Confused, I stated the truth again. "I gave candy."

The last thing I remember was sitting in a corner, and that I was forbidden to ride the tricycle.

"Do you remember now?" my mom asked.

I smiled. "Yes. I remember you were talking to the teacher and you took me home. I think that was the last time I went to that preschool."

"That's right. You made all the children believe you had candy for them."

"Well, I remembered you telling me it was candy."

"No, I didn't. You thought everything was candy. I just want you to remember to stop passing out drugs to little children."

"Well, it's kind of hard. You know, candy is a form of drugs," I chuckled.

She gave me an *ahjumma* stare—which was an emotionless facial expression that made the observer wonder if she was happy, sad, joking, or angry. "Just remember, you're dangerous."

"Okay Mom." I gave her a hug. Hugging was a physical gesture to make my situations lighthearted.

I was the dangerous one. This was another label that I had been given, one that I had to choose or reject as I got older. I chose to reject it, but held onto the idea that I was the ringleader who had power when I spoke. My words pierced people's hearts and minds.

Academic Learning

Comprehending what I read was frustrating. When I read, I often fell asleep or glanced over the words. The passages I read were incomprehensible, and I had to go back and reread the words. I often wondered if I had a reading problem. I read out loud very well in elementary school, so my teachers never caught on to my reading issues. Year after year, the textbooks became harder to understand. I needed help, and I had to find the root cause.

I began to realize why reading was a heavy task for me. I grew up getting into trouble a lot from my parents because I was supposedly "funny." I would do pranks and make a mess around the house. As I was more like the "boy" in the house, I climbed the bedroom walls, jumped off stairs, and climbed trees. This was not appropriate behavior for a Korean female; I wasn't supposed to be a wild girl. As a result, I got punished for my antics. Many times, Dad put me in the corner of the room. I had to face the wall, kneel down, and raise my hands in the air.

"Stay like that," he said in a stern voice. He then put a heavy book or books on my palms.

"Keep it straight," he would say. "You need to learn how to behave."

He explained that this was the way he got punished in Korea.

"*Appa*, this is not Korea. This is America!" I exclaimed. My skinny arms could not handle holding the books up in the air, and I often remembered bending my elbows.

"Keep your arms up and straight!" He would sternly warn me.

"I am sorry."

"For what?"

"For disobeying you!" I cried out.

"Are you going to do it again?" he demanded.

"No, no, no. I won't. I promise," I pleaded.

However, this never lasted long. Soon enough, I would make the same mistakes and be back in my corner with the books.

They became my arch-enemies, which probably contributed to my hatred of books. And reading.

Now, I often tell people that I grew up embracing books.

"I've embraced Shakespeare, the classics, encyclopedia, and the Bible while growing up," I tell them.

"Wow, you must love reading," Beth once said.

"Not really. I don't like books."

"Well to have embraced such books requires a lot of patience and perseverance."

"Yes, it did. It sure did. I have gotten stronger and was able to embrace more books, especially heavier books."

When it came to academics, I learned to get by in order to avoid being punished at home or at afterschool tutoring centers. Understanding what I was learning did not come naturally for me, but my classmates and teachers thought I was "innately" smart. But they didn't know what went on behind the scenes to get my study skills together, especially in science and math. . . and in English, history, and writing. They only saw me as the smart Korean girl.

Every time my third grade teacher played "Around the World" using multiplication problems, I always won. 6 x 7 = 42, 12 x 12 = 144, and 12 x 6 = 72. As I was the only Korean student, despite a half-Korean/half-white girl in my class, I was seen as the intelligent Chinese girl. I would be done with my math problems very quickly, ahead of everyone. But they couldn't have known that I had spent countless hours crouching in my closet, underneath my bed, or in the bathroom hiding from my parents and frantically memorizing the multiplication chart. I didn't understand the concepts, but memorized the numerical signs out of sheer fear and desire to not get punished.

One morning Janice, Frank, and I stood next to the multiplication chart. My dad said a few numbers and we had a difficult time formulating the right answers.

"Why can't you get the numbers fast? When I was your age or younger, I was able to answer the math problems."

"It's hard," we would say.

I guess he finally got fed up with us.

"Don't come out until you memorize the multiplication table!" He pushed us into a small, dark closet as punishment. He said he would continually put us there until we could quickly multiply numbers up to 144. I was afraid of the dark. In the beginning, I cried and asked to be released from my dungeon. But I had no choice. Either I had to memorize the numbers quickly or I would get into trouble again.

I eventually became the number one student for "Around the World," but I didn't give my dad credit for this.

On the surface, people perceived that I was innately smart. I didn't understand why they thought Asians were naturally smart, but this assumption certainly helped me. My teachers never said negative comments to me, and I liked the positive encouragement. I didn't want to be labeled as the "lazy, you're dumb, you can't learn fast" student because it was sad when teachers said negative comments to other minority students. My classmates either liked me because I helped them with their work, or they were upset at me for being the "favorite" or "smart."

Being Korean and playing the role as the "smart" student pressured me at school as well as at home. I didn't think of myself as smart, and my dad knew I wasn't innately smart. I was the middle child who struggled and had to get back up when life was difficult, because I was Sarai. I was either going to move forward or get in trouble.

When junior high came around, I did well in school. Faye Ross Middle School had diverse groups of African Americans, Latina/o students, Asian American Pacific Islander students, and whites. The classes were easy. I discovered if I completed my homework on time, I would get A's in my classes. This was my method of succeeding in school. I didn't understand why some of the students decided to get poor grades. All they needed to do was finish their homework.

However, when I transitioned from middle school to high school, the population became far less diverse. Most of the students at my high school were Asian. Since I had taken honor courses in junior high, I decided to challenge myself by taking honors courses in high school.

During the first few days in class, I had no idea what my teacher was talking about.

"This is the sun and the plant. The plant lives because of photosynthesis," my biology honors teacher stated.

Photo-what? The word was long and either the concept or teaching style was confusing. I looked around to see if I was the only one who was lost. The other Asian students were nodding their heads as if they understood this information. In English class, I was instructed to write an essay. From elementary until middle school, I didn't remember ever writing an academic essay. I went to an urban elementary school and we colored, completed worksheets, and handed in various homework assignments. My teachers from middle school didn't teach me how to write an essay.

I realized I was not as smart as I had thought and that I was ill-prepared for high school. I went to my counselor and changed my honor courses to regular classes. Previously, I had used my ability to complete homework assignments as a measure of my intelligence in schools, but this school was different. I needed to study as well as complete homework assignments.

My Asian face was the poster child for academic excellence, but I was far from it. Sometimes, I got away with my low grades because I was Korean. If I didn't do well on my assignments, my teachers would ask me if they were not challenging enough. Other times, teachers let me make up assignments under the presumption that I had more important functions to fulfill. Sometimes, it was the opposite. Some teachers purposely made assignments more difficult for me because of my outer appearance. Either way, I, like many Asians, was the model minority–a label I wished to never have had.

Korean Hambeogeo

In elementary school, Mom packed Korean lunches for me. I used to take my *dosilak* and eat food out of my lunch box. The food I ate was not of concern until I got a little older, when the reactions of my second grade peers during my *kimchi* days mortified me. Rice and lots of garlic-infused *banchans* aired my elementary classroom.

"Eww, what's that smell?" A student said after I had discreetly opened my lunchbox.

"It smells like fart!" Another student yelled as he pinched his nose.

"No, it's . . . it's Sarai's weird food smell!" Pointed another classmate.

"Ewww!!"

Other people brought American food or purchased the school lunch, and here I was, the only Korean in my classroom with Korean food. I quickly ate my rice, *kimchi*, and other *banchans*, and shut my mouth.

The pungent odor in my class was similar to my dragon breath–or so my classmates told me. Listening to their comments made me self-conscious about my breath and the food I brought to school.

At home, Mom made Korean food for us. I was thankful to have food on the table, but as I became more Americanized, Korean food seemed too cultural. I wanted American food. A budding elementary student knew it was cool to be an American, because that was what was told to me by teachers and other non-Asian students.

"Mom, can we eat American food like a hamburger or sandwich at home?"

"*Weh?*" She inquired.

"Well, other people eat American food. Can't we eat hamburgers or sandwiches?"

"No. At home, you eat Korean food because you are Korean. You have to eat real food."

Even though Mom prepared *dosilak* for me to take to school,

I had hoped she would at least make me a sandwich or hamburger at home. But, I decided, she was definitely trying to brainwash me to be more Korean. As if attending Korean school, being told to speak in Korean, and bowing to adults were not enough.

There were days I ate food at home without complaining, but when I was mocked for eating smelly Korean food at school, my ungrateful attitude came to the surface.

"I don't want to eat Korean food! I hate it! I hate being Korean!" I screamed.

"Be thankful you at least have food on your table. Some people can't eat, and you, who receive royal foods, need to be grateful. You're an ungrateful child. Where did you learn this behavior?"

Pouting and tears rolling down my eyes, I couldn't tell Mom what had been happening to me at school. Here I was, the only person in my class eating packed lunch, while my friends gave the cafeteria lady a yellow ticket to eat school lunches. I didn't know at the time that almost all of my elementary friends were low-income and received free school lunches. Our family barely qualified, and so my parents chose to pack my siblings and me lunches to save money.

I often regretted yelling at my mom because those were days I didn't get to eat. I would stomp away from the kitchen and go into my room to pity myself. After crying profusely for being born Korean, my mind would wander into thinking about my favorite Korean seasoned meats, *galbi* and *bulgogi*. Peace usually came over me as I imagined the sizzling sounds and the sweet and savory tender meat. During those short musings, I reminded myself to enjoy my Koreanness because we Koreans had *galbi* and *bulgogi* to boast about.

One day, wiping my tears after such an outburst, I swallowed excess mucous that clumped in my nostrils and throat. It tasted like *bulgogi*. Thinking about Korean meat was affecting my reality. My room had begun to smell like soy sauce, sugar, onions, *bulgogi*. Taking a few more sniffs, my room was, in fact, filling up with the smell of Korean meat. Mom was making *bulgogi!*

Opening my door and taking small steps so as to not make any noise, I peered into the kitchen to see the meat sizzling on the frying pan. To my left was the kitchen table with no *banchan*. Usually, mom placed the *banchans* on the table before the *gogi* came out. Today was different. She didn't have the *banchan* or the rice out on the table, and I immediately thought Janice forgot to help her. I was taken aback and confused. I looked questioningly at Janice and Frank, who were already seated at the table, but they just shrugged their shoulders.

"Come eat," Mom said. She didn't seem mad or upset.

I hesitated. I wanted to be upset at Mom, but my stomach yearned to eat the meat. I sat in my chair, hunched over, battling to look upset while internally happy to eat *bulgogi*.

"Today is a special day," she said. She plopped a plate in front of me. "*Hambeogeo.*"

A pile of *bulgogi* was sandwiched between two white Wonder Bread slices. There was no American meat, lettuce, tomatoes, pickles, or sauce.

Tensing my body because of Mom's misunderstanding of "hamburger," I informed her, "Mom, you are supposed to put American meat in the white bread, not *bulgogi*," I told her. My siblings also agreed.

"Bread and meat. Meat. *Bulgogi*. You wanted an American *hambeogeo*. I give you a Korean *hambeogeo!*"

"This is weird. You don't mix Korean and American food together," I muttered. I didn't want to continue arguing with my mom about what food items went with what because she was the cook in the house, and I was hungry. Not sure what to make of my Korean American meal, I took a tiny bite. The bright, flavorful fusion of white bread and Korean meat was something I'd never tasted before. It was a wonderful balance.

"Mommy! This is really good! How did you think of this?" I asked.

"Korean American style." She beamed. "You like?"

"I like." Though my tiny stomach had a difficult time eating a whole bowl of rice, finishing my Korean *hambeogeo* was not a problem.

"Thank you. This is delicious," said Janice. Frank didn't say anything, but was busily chowing down on the *hambeogo*.

"Mom, I'm sorry," I mumbled under my breath. "*Mian hae . . .yo.*" I used the honorific ending when I was sorrowful.

She came over, gave me a hug, and then patted my head. I didn't like the pat, but I sure liked the hug. "Korean *hambeogeo*," she said again. "I'm Korean American, too."

Combining two cultural foods did not cross my mind until my mom, the royal chef, taught me to bridge my Korean and American sides by blending the best of both worlds to create something new and better. Eating *Bulgogi hambeogeo* was all I needed. Ever since my mom fused Korean and American cultural foods together, I grew up believing she told the restaurant owners and chefs that blending various spices and dishes from different worlds was the next food craze wave. I attribute all the fusion foods that sprang up throughout the decades to my mom and the many moms who taught their children to love their unique selves.

K-Pop and Dramas

Perceiving myself to be more American, I avoided listening to Korean music. I assumed an American needed to assimilate to mainstream American movies, American TV shows, and American pop music. I thought if I listened to K-pop, I would be labeled as a Korean FOB. Because I didn't want to be associated with this group, I valued American music more than Korean music. At the time, I didn't imagine that "American" media and culture was actually a mix of many ethnicities, cultures, and stories.

My distant heart towards Korean music, culture, and language began to cave in when my high school counselor suggested I take a new foreign language course–Korean.

"You should consider taking Korean as your foreign language course. Our school is piloting this class," my counselor stated. "Let me know what you think about this course."

"No." I said flatly. "What other foreign language courses can I choose for that period?"

"Latin. But I think you should consider taking Korean as your foreign language. Do you speak Korean?"

"Can I take Latin? Hmm. I speak *Konglish*. I have a hard time understanding in Korean. Then again, I have a hard time communicating with my parents. Now that I think about, I don't speak in Korean or *Konglish*."

"Well, this will be good for you. Learning Korean will help you communicate with your family."

She enrolled me in Korean class without further waiting for my permission. I sat at my counselor's office staring at the wall. *Why was she asking me to take Korean?* Past memories of Korean school flooded my mind. Sitting in the corner raising my hands, getting in trouble, and writing the Korean alphabet over and over again . . . these memories made me shiver. My body tensed, and I felt pain in my stomach. And then, unwanted tears welled up in my eyes. I looked away from my counselor so she wouldn't see them.

I took a few deep breaths. *Would learning Korean help me*

communicate with my parents? I envisioned having a delightful conversation with my parents. We spoke and understood each other. We empathized with each other. I smiled and my stomach pain went away. *I can learn Korean and strengthen my relationship with my parents,* I thought. I hoped my *Konglish* skills would help me get by in class, and that the class would help me heal from my painful Korean school memories.

Most of the students in my class were Korean. There were many Korean wangstas, second generation Korean Americans, a few FOBs, one mixed Korean/White student, and one token white student who had some kind of Asian fetish. Most of us enrolled in Korean class with the hope of receiving an "A" because we were Korean. I admit, my Korean Level 1 class was not difficult. The information I learned consisted of the Korean alphabet, the very same letters I wrote multiple times when I was punished during my Korean school days.

Our Korean teacher, Mrs. Lee, was credentialed to teach a different subject, but because she was the only teacher who was Korean, the principal asked her to teach our class. I'm not sure she liked teaching Korean, and looking back, I feel bad for our token Korean teacher.

We were disobedient Korean students. We didn't respect her. We talked out loud, didn't raise our hands when we spoke in class, made fun of each other and her, and walked around the room when she told us to sit and listen. We were unruly Korean children who strayed away from the Confucian principles of honoring our adults. When we were taught to bow, we joked around and nodded our heads instead of bowing our upper body 45-90 degrees.

We had a great time learning Korean bad words even though it was not in our Korean Level 1 book. We got away with it. In addition, when we learned to use *jondaemal*, we didn't take it seriously. Learning *jondaemal* was a challenge because I didn't use it at home or with Korean adults. Some of the wangstas overemphasized the *jondaemal* endings, mocking the honorific form. I was no different from the wangstas; I disrespected *jondaemal*.

Mrs. Lee also wanted to expose us to the Korean culture, which included music and drama. A handful of us mocked the Korean language and the customs, but our teacher would not relent.

She stated we needed to improve our Korean language skills by watching Korean music videos and dramas. We received extra credit if we did.

Being a poor user of *jondaemal* and in need of extra credit, I exposed myself to Korean media. One night, I decided to sit with Dad after he had watched the Korean news, even though my custom was to go straight to my room after our family ate dinner, not re-emerging again until the morning. After the Korean news, a music video usually played on television. Although I didn't know what they were singing about, I mocked their song and dance routine.

"Look how dorky they look. This is horrible. I'm so embarrassed!" I exclaimed.

Mom told me to be quiet, but I couldn't help it. They looked stupid, and their outfits and dance moves didn't help. With a disgusted look on my face, I mentally compared the Korean music video I was watching to the many MTV music videos I frequently watched. The American music videos and songs were far better than what I was watching, far better. I was ashamed of my culture.

To my dismay, the more I was exposed to watching Korean music videos, the more I became addicted to the songs. I didn't want to tell anyone, because I didn't want to admit I was becoming Korean; I didn't want to admit that the rhythmic beats and melodies were actually good. Although the Korean female and male singers looked like stick figures and wore weird clothes, no matter how much I tried to run away from K-pop, I seemed to be drawn in by their melodies, beats, and simple dance moves.

There was one time when I nodded my head to follow the rhythmic beats. I caught myself and looked around to see if anyone had seen me. Behind closed doors, I replayed the Korean songs in my head, and I mimicked their dance moves. No one knew. It would have been embarrassing if people knew I danced in my room to Korean music.

I came to discover that Korean music was popular at my school, mainly because many Asian students were Koreans. Some of the Koreans who immigrated to America when they were young, the 1.5 gens, liked K-pop, and there were a handful of second-generation students who became crazy K-pop fans. In the

90s, DJ Doc, Solid, Fin.K.L, Seo Taiji & Boys, H.O.T., Jinusean, S.E.S., and 1TYM were some of the music groups in Seoul that became very popular in America. H.O.T. members wore huge white gloves, and some students came to school wearing them. If people, both Koreans and non-Koreans, proudly came to school with white, puffy gloves, I knew K-pop was going to be a huge hit.

Like my secret enjoyment of K-Pop, I also pretended to not like Korean dramas. Whenever we discussed K-dramas at school, the students in my Korean class showed an outward disdain for them.

"It's the same plot," Suzi criticized.

"Yea, you totally know what is going to happen," agreed Sarah.

"Some protagonists have cancer and die, young couples have a difficult relationship but end up getting married, there's always the evil scheming mother-in-law, two males who love the same woman who's beneath their social status, and etc.," Jim, the smart wangsta, chimed in.

"Yeah, and to top it off, their facial features don't move," Suzi responded. "When they're happy, sad, or depressed, their faces stay the same. The only difference is the tears that roll down their cheeks."

"Plastic surgery! The actresses practically look the same!" exclaimed Sarah.

"But for some reason, I can't help but watch K-dramas. Knowing the plot and what is going to happen, I still watch them. It's addicting." Jim confessed his obsession for K-dramas. He came out.

When it came to Korean dramas, I had my own treacherous plot. I never knew that I had an addictive personality until I watched my first Korean drama. I believe they put MSG in the dramas to make them addicting. After each episode, I was drawn to watch the next one, and the next, and the next.

One of the pivotal dramas that ignited my desire to watch Korean dramas was in 1997 when *Star in My Heart* (*Byeol-eun Nae Ga-seum-e*) was playing on television. When it aired, it be-came a hit. The most prized Korean actress was Choi Jin Sil, a woman who eventually committed suicide in real life. Cha In Pyo and Ahn Jae Wook were two male actors who played pivotal roles in the series. Ahn's character drove a sky blue BMW Z3 roadster that was rare to see in K-dramas. I was in awe over the BMW because I never saw anything like it.

The drama was so popular with Koreans that someone from my school came in the same baby blue car a few months after the drama aired. I was surprised to see people actually take K-drama addiction to another level. Secondly, I was flabbergasted that someone had the money to buy a new Z3.

Star in My Heart captured my heart, and my iciness towards Korean media thawed. In addition, my heart began to befriend my parents when I spent time watching Korean shows with them. Although they said I should not watch television because I needed to study, they didn't object when it came to Korean dramas. This was our way of spending quality time—sitting together in a room, not talking about our personal lives, and watching television. It was good enough.

My parents may have believed our time watching Korean shows was family-oriented. Their way of communicating with me was when they translated what was happening during a particular scene, even though English subtitles were on the television screen. Dad had to comment and inform me what was going on.

"The king said he liked the concubine," he would say.

"Dad, I just read that."

"The lights went out and the king and the concubine went into the room."

"Dad, I just saw that."

"The concubine is pregnant."

"Dad, I see that."

Some K-dramas on television didn't provide English subtitles. It was then that we communicated in Korean.

"*Juh-guh moh ya?*" I asked *what is that?* with my poor Korean skills. No answer. "*Moh yeh gi heh suh?*" I asked *what did they say?* No answer. I asked again and received no response. They were so glued to the drama that they ignored me.

"Mom, what are they saying? I don't understand. Please help. What did the guy say? Wait, what is happening now?"

"The lady is the lawyer's mom. Mr. Kim killed her," my mom

briefly stated during the commercials. Sigh. The intense scene ended a while back, and she only gave me a simple gist of what happened. During the intense scenes, I was frustrated because my heart would beat rapidly, but I had no idea what the actors were saying to each other. It was frustrating.

Whether my parents did this on purpose or not, I learned how to be patient and master deferred gratification when I watched dramas with no English subtitles. I had to watch particular scenes first and then learn what they said during commercial breaks. This pattern reminded me of Bruce Lee's movies when the actors voices were delayed after their mouths were moving.

My love for K-dramas increased, and so did computer technologies, alongside Korean video stores that rented out a variety of K-dramas. I stumbled across websites that had links to various K-dramas and K-movies available for download and online viewing. These websites shaped me into a real addict by giving me access to watching multiple series on my computer rather than waiting to watch another episode on television.

Like every good addict, I had a method. I opened four to five tabs and had each window tab uploading the next sequential episode. After I was done with one episode, I prepped the fifth episode on the fifth tab, which would download completely by the time I got to it. I then would immediately watch the following episode from the second tab. This system worked very well because I was able to see the episodes back to back, so I could finish the drama faster. I ended up watching way too many K-dramas and K-movies.

The blessing of technology soon became a curse. I couldn't stop watching. I watched dramas until I fell asleep, and sleeping wasn't by choice. My body shut down and my eyes wouldn't open anymore. For days, I watched dramas, and I could not function during the day. I became ill because my body wasn't getting enough sleep. How could I sleep when there were so many K-dramas to watch?

Watching K-dramas became a real problem in my life, and I had to make a pivotal decision and stop watching—cold turkey. When my fingers wanted to go to the K-drama sites, I told my hands to stop. Although I wanted to watch dramas with my parents, I avoided it. I went to my room immediately after eating dinner and shut my door. Although I reduced my K-drama addiction, I ended up distancing my relationship and lost the K-drama connection with my parents. It was unfortunate, but I needed to become healthy again. Once I learned how to control my addiction to K-dramas and continued to take Korean classes throughout my high school years, I began to build a relationship with my parents without using T.V. as a medium. We actually talked.

Interestingly enough, their stories were better than any Korean dramas I saw on television; and we were the characters.

You're Pretty Only if You Keep Your Mouth Shut

"Ho ho ho ho. Smile when you say ho ho ho," my mom frequently said every time I laughed. "Korean females should be ladylike." Mom often scolded me to be docile and "feminine" in my manners. Especially when it came to my laughter.

"Mom, I can't laugh like you. It's too funny, and it sounds fake. Can't I laugh my way?"

"No," she firmly stated. "When you laugh, your teeth show, your saliva is dangling in your mouth, and you look unattractive. If you keep laughing like that, other mothers will think I didn't train you well, and you won't get married."

I couldn't help that my laugh was very peculiar.

"You're a machine gun-woody woodpecker," Frank said to me. "You sound like a machine gun. It's funny because you look funny when you laugh like that."

Though perhaps quite unattractive and expressing poor table manners, my machine-gun laugh was hard to stop once it started, and it was contagious—especially when I ate with friends. I would open my mouth full of food with food particles between my teeth. Next, I nodded my head fervently up and down while turning my head from one side of the table towards the other side. Pretty soon the table full of friends would be laughing right along with me.

Mom reprimanded me. "A Korean female needs to close her mouth, turn to the side, and say 'ho ho ho.' I keep telling you to stop laughing like this. You have *gochu* (red pepper) and *sangchu* (lettuce) between your teeth. You are absolutely disgusting and gross."

"So," I let out a burp.

"How are you going to get married when you laugh like that and have poor table manners? *Aigoo!*" She left the kitchen disappointed and discouraged.

"Don't worry. I'll find someone who likes my laugh and loves me for who I am," I reassured my family. My family members

129

gawked at me.

"If you don't change your habits now," warned Mom, "they'll become permanent in the future. Change is important. As you change, you become pretty."

"Mom, you said I was pretty because I'm your daughter. I'm a powerful princess!"

"*Aigoo*," Mom said. "You are pretty because you're my daughter, but other people won't think the same way. Keep your mouth shut and laugh like a woman."

Besides my mom trying to teach me to be lady-like and keep quiet, others chose to teach me as well. Apparently, I had more to fix than just my obnoxious laugh.

"You're pretty—only if you keep your mouth shut. You got big lips," Janice told me.

"Why do you say that?" I asked. During my adolescence, my facial features were disproportionate. Literally, I had big lips.

"Well, you're pretty. But for some reason, when you open your mouth, what you say, how you say it, and your facial expressions make you look so ugly."

"I'm not sure if this is a compliment or an insult." My lips protruded out and downward.

"It's an insult and compliment," she smiled. "Haven't you noticed you make friends very quickly and lose them once you open your mouth?" This was somewhat true. When I opened my mouth, some people slightly leaned away from me. It may have been my garlic breath or my way of conveying words.

But, it wasn't my breath or my actual big lips. What came out of my mouth was often the determining factor that alarmed people. When people asked for my feedback about how they look, what I thought about an issue, or what they should do, I told them the truth.

"You're so judgmental," Annie once said to me.

"Why don't you be more tactful if you're going to open your mouth," Bryan sternly reprimanded me. I didn't know why he told me to be more tactful when he and other students said whatever they wanted. It was okay if they made comments with less tact because I didn't mind, but when it was my turn, they weren't too happy with me.

Pointing a chef's knife towards me, Mom said, "You need to

be tactful in how you say things." She turned her body away from me and began chopping carrots into thin slices. Maybe she needed to be tactful in the way she pointed sharp objects.

"How?" I inquired.

"You need *noonchi*."

"*Noonchi?* I have it. *Noon* means eyes."

"Aigoo."

Trying to be funny didn't work with Mom.

"Mom, what if an outfit didn't look good on the person, but she liked it? What do I say? I usually say it looks ugly and the person gets upset or offended at me. Why did the person get upset at me when she asked for my opinion?" I tactfully leaned over and ate some of her carrot slices.

"She didn't ask you," Mom stated.

"Yes, she did. She asked me a question." Rolling my eyes upward, I perceived my mom wasn't hearing me.

"That's my point. She asked you a question, but she, in fact, didn't ask you."

"Yes, she did. I just told you." There must have been a communication problem with Mom. "She asked me a question regarding my opinion."

"Exactly. She asked you a question, but she really didn't." Mom probably saw I was getting frustrated with her responses.

"Look," she continued, "when people ask you a question for your opinion, you need discernment. There's a reason why people ask you a question. You need to find the purpose as to why they do. They either want your support and encouragement, really want you to answer their questions, or something else. Read between the lines. Have some *noonchi*."

"Then why ask a question if she doesn't really want my opinion? Okay, for example, if my friend asked me how an outfit looks like, what should I say?"

"You can say, 'What do you think?' Or, you can say, 'Why don't you ask other people in the store?'"

"Then I'll be redirecting my answers to the person who asked the question or to someone else."

"This is art. Many politicians and high-powered people do this," Mom shared.

"Yes, but, I'm not them. I want to be truthful and respond

when asked."

"Redirecting your responses does not mean you didn't an-swer them. You gave them options beyond your limited mind. Anyway, be thoughtful and make sure you don't hurt people's feelings, especially your siblings." She sliced the firm tofu into pieces.

"Mom, when a lady with a perm went to the restroom, I no-ticed a group of Korean ladies talk badly about the woman. They said the lady's hair looked fried and frazzled. When the lady with the perm came back from the restroom, the ladies said, 'Oh, you got a perm. It looks great.' Mom, these people lied in front of the lady. I think this is wrong."

"Yes, and it is best to not say anything. Keep your mouth shut. A Korean female should learn to be quiet and smile. You look mad when you don't smile." Her comment didn't have any-thing to do with the story I had previously shared. There was no connection to lying in front of people and keeping my mouth shut and smiling.

"Why do Korean females have to keep quiet?" I questioned. "How come I can't open my mouth and say whatever I want to say? Korean males and older people say whatever is on their minds. Who made up this rule? A man can speak, but women and young people are told to keep their mouths shut." None of this made any sense, and my frowning duck-lips protruded.

Partly frustrated from miscommunication and language bar-riers with Mom, I proceeded, "Mom, I still remember an incident in Korean school in elementary school. Can I tell you? The Ko-rean School director's daughter was one of the oldest students.

She was tall, skinny, and bossy. Since I was small, I decided to go about my way and be invisible so I wouldn't be picked on."

"Okay." Mom was putting ingredients in a pot full of water.

"Well, for a while, the director's daughter and her friends made fun of this other Korean girl who wore glasses and looked a little overweight. They just picked on her. On some days, she had the girl with glasses do things for her."

"And?"

"One day when school was out and I was waiting for you, the director's daughter was playing with the girl's hair. The girl sat on the cement floor right in front of the gate and the director's daughter and friends were right behind her. Everyone was giggling and smiling. The girl with glasses was smiling because she felt like she was part of the group. However, she didn't know the girls sitting behind her were chewing gum and attaching it to the girl's hair. I saw about 10 pieces of gum placed all over the girl's hair."

"*Oh mae mae* (oh my my)."

"Mom, I looked at this going on, and I wanted to say something because this was wrong. However, the director's daughter put her finger over her lips to tell me to keep quiet. So, I kept quiet."

"No, dear. This is when you should say something."

"Well, that's my problem. I just do and say what people tell me to do. If they want my opinion, I give it. If they don't want me to say anything, I keep my mouth shut. And, you told me earlier to keep my mouth shut."

"Well, in certain cases, you will need to keep your mouth shut and other times you will have to say something. Just have *noonchi*."

Though I desired to shut my ears to my mom's advice, she was right. She was always right, but I didn't like how she scolded and threatened me. Maybe she simply didn't know how to teach me in an encouraging way. I kept my mouth shut about this and chose to figure out how to improve my communication skills, because sooner or later, if I didn't, the manner and words I conveyed towards others would boomerang back at me. If I didn't like hearing critical, negative, or discouraging words, I had to find some positive words to use.

More than keeping my mouth shut, I learned how to shut off discouraging and heart-broken words. The sign of a pretty woman was someone who wisely used her words to bring life and light to people. And, despite the changes I made in my manner of talking, I still kept my obnoxious laugh because it made others laugh too.

But It's Not My Fault

"Apologize to your sister," Mom said.

"But, it's not my fault!" I yelled. My heart was pounding after arguing with my sister, who had cussed at me and made me feel stupid. This time it wasn't my fault. Janice had hogged the TV remote control and changed the channel without asking me. She used her "I'm older" birth order card to do whatever she wanted.

"You're the younger sister. You should *yang-bo*."

"Why give in? Shouldn't the older sister wait and *yang-bo* first? I'm the younger sister."

"Yes, but you're Sarai. Apologize to your sister."

"Why can't she apologize?! Why do I always have to apologize?"

"Because you're the younger sister, and you shouldn't behave the way you do even if she says or does things to you."

Whether I personally felt it wasn't my fault or blatantly knew it was my fault, I always had to apologize. Yet, as each year progressed, I withheld my apologies, stubbornly hoping my sister would apologize first. She was more stubborn than I. If I didn't, tension would mount and all hell would break loose in the house.

"I'm sorry," I murmured in a monotone voice to my sister. The apology wasn't sincere because deep down, I believed she should have said sorry, too.

"Why are you sorry?" My sister said as if to teach me a lesson. Preventing myself from yelling at her again, I explained why I was sorry. At these times, I really wanted her to say sorry for being an unloving older sister to me. The numerous times I argued or got into fights with my sister had increased many layers of bitterness and hatred towards her and for being born second.

"Apologize to your brother," Mom told me.

"But, it's not my fault!"

"You're the older sister. Doesn't matter who's at fault."

"But you tell me to apologize to Janice when it's not even my fault because I'm younger. Frank is younger. Have him apol-

135

logize to me." My logic didn't work with my family. Either I apologized or tension mounted in our household.

Peering into his eyes and with an angry tone, I said, "I'm sorry for hitting you even though you hit me, too."

Frank didn't look at me but played with his toys. He heard me, and his silence was his way of saying it was okay. I stared at him and wished he were a girl. Would Mom have my younger sister apologize to me?

"Say sorry to Dad," Mom scolded.

"Why? It's his fault!"

"He's your dad. You shouldn't talk back."

"But he yelled at me and said all kinds of words I don't like to hear."

"You're the daughter. You shouldn't act the way you do."

"But this isn't fair! Why does he treat me like this!"

"Because he's your dad and he's an adult."

Tears streaming down my face with intense frustration and anger for the unfair way Dad yelled at me, I approached him and softly mumbled, "*Mi. . . an. . . hae. . .yo.*"

He didn't stare at me but looked to the side and began talking about how he was not allowed to talk back to his parents, and that I was rude and had no respect for him. I kept quiet as I wondered if he had any respect for me. If he did, he shouldn't have yelled at me, but rather, talked to me.

Growing up, I was asked to *yang-bo* with my family whenever there was a conflict. Although they themselves were at fault because arguments always involved more than one person, my family members would hardly give in, and if they did, saying sorry was heard on rare occasions.

My family members and I didn't talk about our feelings in a calm manner. Our way of forgiving was through actions, whether cleaning the dishes, staying quiet, or other ways. But for me, I always wanted to hear the words, "I'm sorry for saying or doing X, and I will not do it again."

Outside of the home was not different. Non-family members and acquaintances pointed fingers at me and told me what was wrong, but when I wanted to do the same, I was told my manner, behavior, and way of speaking to people was inappropriate.

Every time I experienced something negative in my life for

being mistreated, blamed, and devalued, a new thin layer of concrete covered my once tender heart and quickly hardened. My ability to easily forgive, care, and love others became more and more difficult with each new concrete layer. I held onto resentment and bitterness because members of my household and people did the very thing they didn't like me to do. Fingers were pointed at me as if I were the bad daughter, sister, or human being, but did they not know that every time they pointed an index finger at me, three fingers pointed right back at them?

My heart hardened, and I pretended not to be hurt by people. I covered my pain with sarcastic jokes, with my tough "don't mess with me" attitude, by holding back from helping people, by not fulfilling chores or tasks when asked, and by making sure I made the other person feel guilty. When I was told to do something right away, I took my time fulfilling what was required or I wouldn't do it at all. My subtle form of retaliation annoyed and frustrated other people.

I had succeeded in using my form of retaliation because I had been hurt; however, when it was my turn to ask people for help, they did the same thing, too. Some people hesitated, stated they were too busy, or verbally questioned why they should consider helping me when I didn't help them. They, too, built resentment towards me. As a result, their actions frustrated me and made me upset, and I would
remind myself not to help that person the next time.

This cycle of rejection, hurt and retaliation happened in many forms of relationships, whether between friends, siblings, family members, teachers and students, employers and employees, and many more. All of us were blaming each other, hurting each other, and creating divisions. Being rejected and rejecting others through various forms of retaliation damaged our well-being and quality of life. I hated this, and I hated myself for succumbing to this cycle. I had three fingers pointing at me every time I hurt others.

Although I didn't have a sudden epiphany, years of experiencing negativity, rejection, and retaliation became unbearable, maybe because I didn't want to end up like the bitter, angry, depressed, and lonely people. These miserable individuals with their frowning faces and negative comments made me realize I needed to stop my childish, negative, retaliating, angry, and irritable attitude and actions.

My first step to emotionally mature as a person was to learn how to forgive others and then myself. Saying sorry and truly meaning it was important when forgiving and being forgiven. Previously, I had thought that apologizing whether I was or was not at fault was a sign of weakness and a loss of my power. However, when I said sorry and truly meant it, I felt a great release of positive power that flowed through my thoughts and feelings towards the other person. The heavy tension in my body and atmosphere lifted, and my body felt light and free.

In addition, I discovered apologies were difficult to give when I thought I wasn't at fault. But the mere fact of my refusal to apologize showed that I really did bear some responsibility for the negative situation. If I believed something that had happened wasn't my fault, then I wouldn't withhold my apologies. When I had discovered why I hesitated, I immediately learned to reframe my thinking to believe that no matter where the fault and blame lie, if the other party was hurt, then it was my responsibility to apologize and take the initiative to restore the relationship.

When people used various forms of rejecting the other person because they were offended or hurt, I did the opposite. I discarded my insecure prideful tendencies by letting go of my pain and forgiving people who had hurt me. I stopped hurting people with my words and actions, stopped holding onto bitterness and past pain, and started saying sorry.

"Shouldn't you get upset at what she did?" A colleague inquired after hearing how a person had harassed and slandered me.

"Why?"

"If I were you, I would have done something to hurt her for hurting you."

"That's a low blow. You can't fight evil with evil, but evil with good. It's best to forgive and love. She has held onto her past pain and hasn't forgiven others and herself. I don't want to become like her by retaliating."

My journey in saying sorry starting from when I was young, has been to value and love others as myself. By truly loving myself, I learned how to forgive others when I was mistreated, devalued, and hated on. Learning to forgive and say sorry were potent weapons to create peace among others and inside my soul. I now share my secret weapon with others whether they choose to forgive or continue to hold onto their past pain, bitterness, and anger.

Mirror Image

"Only you could've experienced this!" Suzi shook her head side to side, smirking. "How could you forget what you look like? Don't you see yourself in the mirror?"

"Yeah . . . but aren't there times you forget how you look? Depending on how much makeup you put on, what clothes you wear, and hairstyle?" Out of millions of people, I couldn't be the only person who experienced this.

"Yes and no, but not really. I know what I look like," Suzi stated.

"Even with all your plastic surgery?" I joked. Suzi rolled her eyes at me.

"I'm pretty sure other people forget how they look," I continued.

"No way, not in college. I think you're going through an identity crisis."

That weekend, Grace and I had gone to a party in Old Town Pasadena because she had wanted to introduce me to her other friends. The dim lights at the restaurant made everyone look great. So great, in fact, that people kept glancing at each other and then at themselves in the mirrors that were placed in various parts of the building. Not wanting to come off as a narcissist, I avoided looking at myself the entire time.

Needing to use the restroom, which was located below, I told the group I would be back. There were many people coming up and down the stairs. Maneuvering my way and nearing the bottom of the step, I noticed an Asian woman. Although I was many miles away from my university, and despite the few Asians who were at the restaurant, I knew she and I went to the same school. Maybe she was in one of the Asian clubs I was involved with because she was smiling at me. She looked pretty with her twisted hair and her stylish outfit. So, I raised my right hand to wave at her, and she waved back. This was great! I walked closer to her, hoping to make small talk and give her a hug.

I ended up touching the mirror. I had been waving at myself, and the "familiar" girl was my own reflection. Mildly embarrassed, I ducked into the bathroom, washed and dried my hands with the towel, and stared at myself in the mirror. There was no alcohol in my system, and I wasn't tired. Though embarrassed, I was quite intrigued that the attractive, Korean female whose hair was twisted, clothes were pretty and fashionable, and makeup looked fabulous, was me.

People have often told me I was beautiful, maybe because of my awesome personality, but I hadn't appreciated my outer attributes as much as I should have. What I didn't like about myself was noticeable. The mirror image of myself often highlighted the freckles on my cheeks, the big pores on my nose after squeezing so many blackheads, my flat nose, blue-tinted baggy eyes, and the sparse hair on my widow's peak.

But that night for the first time, looking at myself in the mirror, I genuinely believed I was beautiful. I hadn't thought positively about myself and other Koreans or Asians because my image of female beauty was women with proportionate, Western features. Smiling in the mirror, I remembered the first time I had run into myself.

Besides moving away from home, matriculating to college was a time of new changes—new friends, environment, classes, etc. I was excited to join new clubs and make new friends. My college was big and so were my dreams. I was free from the constraints of the "Korean" or adult-constructed cultural rules.

On a Saturday morning during my first quarter, I participated in a scavenger hunt hosted by a local church. This event would allow new college students to explore the city and meet new people. One of the tasks was to find items at the University Town Center near my college. People were put into smaller groups to compete for the grand prize. I was given the task of picking up all the menus from the food court. With a goal in mind and wanting to contribute to my team, I hurriedly picked up as many menus as possible. I was good at picking up menus because I was small and quick.

After thinking I picked up the last menu, I turned left and noticed there were more places to eat at the food court. I moved my body towards the side of the food court that I had missed, but I was almost immediately stopped.

A young teenager was blocking my way. *Did she not want*

me to win the game? She was about my height, with no makeup, but much younger than I. *She has some nerve*, I thought.

I moved a little to the left, and she moved in the same direction. I moved right and she followed. Because I was older, I thought this girl to be rude and inconsiderate for not allowing me the right to pass. I grew agitated. Looking deeply into her eyes, I tried to scorn her. But she still didn't budge.

For some reason, I thought about a lesson we'd learned in Korean class about how younger people shouldn't look at their elders in the eyes. Previously, I had thought that was ridiculous because in the American culture, people looked at each other. I looked at people in the eyes whether they were children, adults, or Koreans.

However, at this moment, I felt like a Korean adult who needed to scorn and discipline this young lady whose piercing eyes didn't blink when she stared at me. Before telling this young lady that I demanded respect and honor because I was older than she, I paused and recollected myself. Growing up, I disliked how people misused their power and control just because they were older, richer, smarter, or whatever. I had prayed to God that I would not become an ignorant adult who perpetuated the systemic issues I so disdained.

Being Korean and connected to almost everyone within two degrees of separation, I assumed the girl staring at me was someone I knew. I quickly went through my mental Rolodex of people from my past.

Oh yes! She had gone to my high school! I guess she was stopping me because she wanted to say hi--or, hey! She had menus in her hand, and she might be playing the scavenger hunt game, too. Internally ashamed for judging her, I slightly smiled to let her know I knew her. Her demeanor immediately changed, and she smiled back. I raised my hand and approached her.

Unfortunately, my greeting was cut short. My nose touched the mirror. I had been scorning myself.

Though my two mirror incidences were more than bloopers, these atypical events tremendously impacted my life. My first mirror encounter alerted me to the fact that I had done the very thing that I criticized others for doing. The judgment, control, and demand for respect were the very ideologies that were embedded in my soul, no matter that I had fiercely opposed them. Despite being a fresh college student, I made the pivotal decision to reassess the way I was going to think internally regarding my treatment of others. In order to transform myself and become the person I so desired, someone who loved others on the inside and outside, I needed to counter what society and media were teaching me.

When I excitedly greeted myself in the mirror the second time, I knew that I had become the person I wanted to become. I not only rediscovered the value of my outer Korean beauty, but also learned to value, appreciate, and love others as myself. The mirror was one of the greatest learning tools in helping me discover how we can be changed for the better.

My Heart Says Yes But I Say No

"You must have dated a lot and had a lot of boyfriends," a male friend informed me in my 30s.

I smiled. "Not really. Not as much as you think."

"What? With your looks, personality, and education? You're a great catch."

"Well, my mom says my education, looks, and personality are too much. She said I need to act dumb, so I wouldn't intimidate men because of my degrees, wear less makeup so I wouldn't scare men when I didn't wear any, and look and act feminine to attract them. My sister says I look feminine until I open my mouth. I just think the men are insecure. Why would I have to act less smart just so I can catch the attention of men?"

"You need to find yourself a confident gentleman."

"Where are the gentlemen?" I smiled at my male friend who was already dating someone else. Even if he were single, I wouldn't have dated him.

I had liked many guys in elementary school, high school, college, or thereafter, but that was about it. Securing a boyfriend was difficult. My sister attributed my lack of experience to my inability to be flirtatious. When many females flirted by slightly touching men with their hands, giggling, flipping their hair, or giving their treasure chest away, I didn't do any of that. She said I went on dates as if they were business meetings, interviewing them to recruit them as a potential business partner or an assistant. She didn't know how I acted and spoke with men, but maybe she was right. I told her I'd rather not flirt the "girly way" because it was too awkward and fake. Plus, I couldn't let the guys know I was interested in them, and if I did, I used my non-flirting tactics.

In elementary, I punched guys, arm wrestled, and played handball with the boys I had a crush on. In junior high, I chased the boys and punched their arms to show how strong I was. In high school, I stopped punching their arms and competing with them in sports. They had gotten their growth spurt. Rather, I chose to glance at my crushes from the corner of my eyes and secretly hope I would catch their attention. It didn't work.

One approach that was successful was to get set up by a friend. Jan, who went to high school with Jason, had set us up during my first or second year in high school. Jason and I had talked on the phone a couple of times, and we scheduled our first face-to-face meeting at Jan's house. My mom dropped me off thinking I was going to only hang out with my friend. I did, plus one more.

My heart pounded from nervousness and excitement. He had dated before, but for me, this was my first time, so I tried to remain calm. When I saw his dark brown eyes, square face, and spiky hair, I knew I'd hit the jackpot.

Not knowing what to do, Jan, Jason, and I strolled around the block and talked. We were both nervous, but he showed it. He tripped over little cracks, and when we were around the corner of the house, he ran towards the door so fast that he slipped and fell in front of us. He got up quickly and pretended he did it on purpose. We were both interested in each other. We wrote letters and talked to each other on the home phone.

"Do you want to be my girlfriend?" Jason asked one day.

Energy surged through me. A guy who liked me actually asked me out. Yes! I told myself. I imagined getting chocolate and flowers on Valentines, hugging, holding hands, and having my first kiss with him. I was ready for my first boyfriend.

As I was about to say yes, I heard a voice, possibly coming from the center of my belly. It was definitely not my voice because it said, "No, you're not ready." This voice was God. When I heard God say no, He then showed me flashes of my future relationship with Jason. I saw myself getting into an argument with him, crying, and then breaking up with him. Though my hormones, heart, and mind wanted to say yes, God knew this relationship wasn't for me.

With a mixture of sadness and hesitation, I told Jason, "I can't. Not right now."

He took my latter response with hope because he pursued me again the following year. However, my answer stayed the same. Later, I discovered that he was a player, and I was grateful that I had turned him down. I didn't want to be a number on his list. In the following years, I would run into him randomly in places like New York, San Diego, and Washington D.C. At one point he told me I was the only girl who had rejected him. I cherished that title with great pride.

After I had said no to Jason, I met and became friends with Sam. He was shy and had nothing really to say, maybe because he was a FOB. So, I did most of the talking. During my senior year, my friends and I went to his house to study, but rather than studying, he copied my math homework. At first, I didn't mind, but later I realized I was getting the short end of the stick. He received better test grades than I. I did the work, and he benefitted.

Though we were friends, we liked each other. It was never stated, but felt. I knew he loved me, and with the ache I felt in my heart when I thought of him, I, too, loved him. We were never romantic with each other, except for a hug or two and a slow dance at the high school formal.

"Do you want to be my girlfriend?" He murmured over the phone during my first quarter in college. Both of us went to different colleges, but we took the time to connect with each other by calling on the phone and paging messages back and forth on our beepers.

Finally, I thought. My initial response was yes. My heart said *YES*. I knew he would take good care of me. However, I was intercepted again.

"No," God internally spoke to me. "He's not the one. You're not ready." He then showed me a vision of what would happen in the relationship. I would be jaded and bored from talking on the phone all the time. Cultural differences would impede us from effectively communicating with each other, and my time finding new friendships in college would diminish. On top of it, my relationship with him wouldn't lead to a blissful marriage.

Crying from the depths of my soul because I wanted to say yes, I said, "I can't." My response reverberated through the coiled phone wires and cut both of our hearts into pieces.

Though I still wanted to be friends, this call was the last time I would get to speak with him for a long time. My answer shattered his heart, which then affected his experience in college.

He was no longer the same person, but a hopeless college student who drank and smoked. After college, I found out that he moved back to Korea.

After a decade had passed, I went to Korea for my brother's wedding. There, I contacted Sam and scheduled a time to meet him. He agreed, and we met at a coffee shop. He was more talkative, but still his shy self. We talked about what we were doing and caught up with life. However, one thing he didn't want to do was talk about us. He tilted his head down as if to erase that painful part of his past while I sat across from him, never telling him that I had deeply cared for him. Although I was never romantically involved with him, my love for him had been genuine.

Though my heart was shattered from my friendship with Sam and Don, a Korean American stud, revived my heart with hot flashes. I was in the second quarter of my first year in college, and good-looking Don lived on the bottom floor of my dorm. Because he was too handsome, I couldn't stare at him directly. I used my peripheral vision to see what he was doing when he was at the dining hall, studying at the lounge, or hanging out with his friends. When he walked by, my heart fluttered. For the first quarter, he didn't notice me, or if he did, he didn't let me know. Wherever I went, there he was with his sky blue baseball cap. I wasn't sure if it was my late night run to the campus store wearing my pajamas with cow prints, eating Ben & Jerry's Funky Monkey or Chocolate Fudge Brownie ice cream at the study lounge, eating massive amounts of food at the food court, making loud burps, or roaming around my large university hanging out with my new friends, but I caught his attention. He spoke to me, and we began to spend time together.

I had no idea he had liked me. He didn't tell me but apparently dropped clues; however, these hints weren't enough to let me know. There were only two incidences I could think of, but I wasn't sure if these were even hints. For example, one day when it was raining, he came under my umbrella and said he liked to share umbrellas with people he liked. I didn't. I liked my big umbrella so it would protect my backpack and me. Sharing the umbrella meant that I got wet. But since it was Don, and he didn't have an umbrella on a rainy day, I didn't mind sharing it with him. Then, on my birthday, he burned his favorite Korean songs onto a CD and gave it to me as a gift. He had printed a picture of Claire Danes on the front CD cover when she was cast as Juliet in *Romeo and Juliet*. Since I didn't have many Korean songs, I was grateful for his present. If these were the "clues," I didn't get them at the time.

The following year, he stopped talking to me. When I spoke to him, he made short comments or was snappy with me. His nice demeanor changed to jerk status.

"Did you not know he liked you?" Jennifer said.

"He liked me? He likes me?" I inquired. "How can this be?"

"He doesn't like you now, but he did. Didn't you get the hints?" she stared at me wondering if I was pretending.

"No. Isn't he nice to everyone? He hangs out with you and the other girls and guys. How did he like me and never tell me?"

"It's *noonchi*. You just know."

Well, I didn't, really. My friendship with Don was short-lived because eventually he didn't want to be near me or be friends. The hope of him asking me to be his girlfriend had passed. I guess I missed my timing or I didn't have *noonchi*. However, if he had really liked me, he should have pursued me until I would say yes. He never did.

"Stop being picky," my friends said during my latter years in college. "Just date."

"Well, is there anyone who's going to ask me?"

"There's plenty of guys who want to ask you."

"Really? Where? And, are they of quality? My style?" Besides being asked by Don to a dance party my first year in college, no one seemed to be interested in me. On the outside, I was the blonde-haired, motorcycle chic who looked promiscuous, but internally, I was the innocent adventurous chic who had never had a boyfriend nor even kissed a guy. Though I dreamt to find my husband in college, I never did.

Whether because something was wrong with me, God preventing me from meeting someone and saying "yes" to him, or simply the lack of quality men on campus, I was a lonely soul looking for my soul mate. I thought the next time someone would ask me I would say yes. I couldn't wait any longer. There were a few times I saw myself living alone with 100 cats, a vision I had hoped would not come true.

When I was 24, I finally spoke to a guy that I had wanted to meet when I first laid eyes on him a year prior. He was a gentle, nice, good-looking Korean man. I asked God, "Please. Let me just meet him once more." Well, God granted my prayer, and I met him the following year. I thought meeting him again was a sign to be with him and possibly marry him. I cherished the idea that the first man I had as a boyfriend would be my husband.

"God, can I please date him? Can he be my husband?" I prayed.

Then, He said, "No." This time, however, instead of complying, I tuned out His voice because I wanted to be with this man. After hearing so many "No's" in my past, I decided maybe God was wrong, and so I pleaded with Him.

"God, I'll be really good, I'll do whatever you want me to do, just let me be with him." I couldn't hold onto my single status any longer. So, when he asked me four months later, I went ahead and said, "Yes." I finally had a boyfriend at the ripe age of 24.

Snagging a handsome man as my first boyfriend was worth celebrating. I envisioned marrying him and living a happy life. With great jubilee, I informed my friends and others that he was the man I was going to marry. We were a cute couple despite our personality differences. I was the energetic wildflower while he was the calm Korean man.

"You'd better watch out," my girlfriend said. "His mom is crazy."

"Don't worry, I'm crazy, too. Did you forget my last name is Koo? I can handle her. He's supposed to be my husband." I received this warning during my first year in the relationship, and I held onto what was shared with me even after seven years had passed, when we finally broke up for good.

Seven years was a long time because both of us, knowing we weren't supposed to remain in the relationship, held onto the hope that it could work out.

God knew better. He was definitely not the person I would marry. Though I wouldn't reverse my time with him, God taught me to not date men like him. Even though he was a nice guy who shared similar beliefs as I did, how we chose to live out those beliefs were too different for me to be truly content in our relationship.

When it was over, many friends said that the healing process would take time, and possibly many years, especially because the relationship was long term. I didn't want to be that person, so I prayed to God to have me heal quickly. I needed the healing process to quicken because I didn't want to be the type of person who held onto bitterness and hurt from her past relationship as well as repeat the same mistakes by dating similar people from my past.

My cousin, sister, and friend told me that there was a common cycle people went through after a breakup: crying, regretting, trying to get back with the person, getting angry, feeling depressed, and more. I applied what they taught me, and so, during the first month, I cried. Mom let me cry from the depths of my soul. She consoled me and told me I had made the best decision.

After crying, I thought about my life without him and about the great times we had shared; I occasionally thought about getting back together with him. This was another stage of the breakup process. However, remembering the decision that I had made, I countered my thoughts and told myself to stop dwelling on him. Reminiscing about my past, about something I wouldn't get back, was a waste of time. The past was the past, and it was time to move forward, to start over, and find someone who would truly value all of me.

After some time, I became very angry and resentful because I had spent seven years with him. That was a long time, and I felt that my twenties were stolen. Now that he was a bachelor, he could date younger women, but my pool of men shrank because I was in my thirties. I prayed to God and pleaded with Him to make me look youthful, to become my energetic self again. I didn't want to become pickled with a sour aftertaste, but a well-preserved woman with great valor. Luckily, with the Korean masks, mom's homemade toner, Korean essence, Korean lotion, and my sister's oil concoctions, my once dry, worn out face looked healthy again.

Some people I knew who broke up with their significant other tried to alleviate their pain by indulging in various activities, binging on various unhealthy foods, or rebounding with other people. I learned that these short-term fixes were not effective, and succumbing to such activities was a sign of my weakness. I chose to remain healthy and avoided dating right after my breakup or do anything that I would regret in the future. Although there were moments when I thought about getting depressed because I was getting old, was lonely and single, I countered my negative thoughts and said, "No!" I reminded myself of my value and worth because I was Sarai, *Mi Kyung*, the powerful princess. Rather than have the "woe is me" attitude, I picked myself up and moved forward to seek new opportunities. God helped me heal, and within two months—even though I had been with him for seven years—I was restored.

One of the important learning tools I used to heal quickly from my long-term relationship was to apply the relationship skills I had taught in classes with youth, singles, couples, married, and divorced couples. As an avid believer of learning and doing, I applied what I had taught others to restore my own soul. For example, one sign of a healed heart is to think the best for my ex. Any negative thought meant I held onto pain. So, when negative words and images crept into my thoughts, I quickly said, "No" and thought of two positive thoughts about him. It worked. In addition, I trained my mind to avoid saying anything negative about him. I kept my mouth shut when people wanted to devalue him, and I prayed to God for his well-being.

People didn't believe me when I told them I was healed. A mutual friend of ours asked, "Are you okay?"

"Why? I'm fine. Why do you ask?"

"Well, are you dating? Are you upset or hurt?

"No, why would I be? I'm waiting to meet someone."

"I don't know how you can handle it? I would be hurt and angry."

"I heal quickly because I learn how to get over relationships. Okay, in actuality, I asked God to take me through the break up and healing process quickly. After two months, I was fine."

"Really? My husband and I thought you'd be upset because, you know he's been dating someone—a white girl."

"Oh my gosh! No way! That's awesome!" With great excitement and shock, hearing him date again was one of the best news I had heard because he stepped out of his comfort zone. I had wished him well, and he, in fact, moved on and found a new love.

In addition, hearing about his new relationship not only made me happy for him, but also made me proud of myself that I genuinely had positive thoughts about him.

I later found out that my sister had helped him decide whether to date the Caucasian girl. Dating her was awesome, but it didn't sit well with me when he went behind my back and received dating advice from my sister. He should have asked his own sister and not mine. Well, I had to forgive him for that because my sister dated diverse people, and his sister didn't. My sister would have been the perfect person to ask for help.

Not being in a relationship has been difficult to explain to my dad when I had to inform him that I needed to wait for God to say yes.

"Have you gone on dates?" My dad asks when he wants to intrude in my personal life.

"Dad, stop worrying." I reassure him.

My mom, a God-fearing woman, understands my circumstance, but on certain occasions, she often stares at me shaking her head side to side. "You shouldn't have gotten your Ph.D."

"What does a Ph.D. degree have anything to do with marriage?" I asked.

"Make sure you don't let the men know you are smarter than they are."

Shaking my head, I said, "Mom, don't worry. My husband who is not insecure will be coming shortly. I don't have to act dumb in order to attract men. Who cares what degree I have. I need to be myself. If he can't handle me, then he shouldn't be with me."

When my mom sees married couples on Korean dramas, she shakes her head and prays out loud, "Jesus, please bring Sarai a husband."

My dad continues to encourage my man-hunt, "Make sure you find a confident man who works diligently." At other times, he asks, "Does Frank have any single friends?"

"Don't worry about it! My husband will come. He's coming soon." I reassure my dad and mom.

"Make sure you act feminine and giggle." Mom said. Dad then teaches me what men like and how women should act.

"Argh! Let me be myself."

Though I avoid having the marriage conversation with my parents, I find myself having similar conversations with friends. "Have you found someone yet?" People, especially my dry cleaners, colleagues, and others ask me. "Don't worry, he'll come." I reassure them. "Make sure you introduce him to us," my Korean dry cleaners couple inform me. They are my second parents who worry about my personal life.

Though my ex was able to date someone else, I wasn't able to find a man to which God said yes. Though I had been set up to meet different men, the answer I received from God was, "No." After making a mistake from my previous relationship, I chose to listen to Him and wait for His "yes" response. God has been gracious and merciful. Rather than saying I'm not ready, He now tells me that He is getting my husband ready. So, I wait patiently.

Flocking to Church

"Time for church!" Mom woke us up.

"Do we have to go?" Janice groaned.

"Of course! We go every Sunday. It's the Lord's Day."

"But, the church told us every day is the Lord's Day," I interjected.

We had no choice. We got ready like many immigrant Korean families in Los Angeles to go to church service. Whether people truly believed in Jesus or not, church was a place where people flocked together to praise God, serve the Lord, make new friendships, establish new business connections, and more. Church was a place where the "Korean culture" was perpetuated whether or not it was based on Biblical principles. Rules were enforced and when not adhered to, consequences followed. I wondered, where was grace and mercy?

"Spit out your gum during church service," a middle-aged teacher told me. He was very hairy, and he shaved his beard twice a day, quite abnormal for Koreans. Chewing gum was a way to prevent my breath from smelling like other people. I couldn't help but desire to give him a piece of my gum.

"Why?" All four-feet and eleven inches of me challenged back.

"Because I said so."

"Well, I like to have gum in my mouth. I don't even chew it or smack on it."

"Well, we need to honor God."

"I honor Him with my heart. Gum has nothing to do with it." Church leaders, it seemed, wanted us to sit erect against the chairs and avoid fooling around during service. It was like school, a place to be conditioned.

"I'm older than you, and I'm a male, and you are not honoring God when you chew gum during service. You need to listen to me. Spit it out, now."

He aired his chest, stared at me, and put his hand out. I spit out my gum on his hand. With disdain for succumbing to his commands, I told myself to not be like that middle-aged hairy man who bossed people around with his puffed heart. He wasn't even the pastor, just an "elder" who volunteered to serve in the youth ministry.

Two things I didn't like. First, when older people used their age as a reason to have younger people listen to them when they themselves didn't uphold their own principles and suggestions. They forgot that they should model their behavior for young people. Second, when people misinterpreted the Bible based on what they liked or disliked, such as creating church rules and regulations based on their own desires and not on God's standard. Then, there was the third.

"This is my daughter. *In-sa heh.*" This last part my mom said to me, nudging me to bow to the adults in front of me.

Nodding my head slightly while looking at them rather than bowing 90-degrees, I quickly stood erect. Sometimes, I stuck out my hand to greet them. Other times, I said hello and smiled. Figuring out how to greet older Korean adults was challenging because I didn't want to bow when my parents and others expected me to do so. During these awkward moments, the adults either laughed and commented on my appearance, or had stern looks on their faces as if I had just disrespected them.

"Hahaha! My daughter was born in the U.S. She is too American and shows no respect. SShhttt." Mom sucked air into her mouth. It sounded like a reverse shit. It was a nonsensical sound that many *ahjummas* made, which often connoted "be quiet" or "you better listen."

"*Ttogbalo In-sa heh.*" Bow correctly. My mom's big fish eyes pierced into mine. I bowed 90 degrees, past 100 degrees, and then quickly ran off. Bowing beyond 90 degrees was my way of mocking the bowing culture to honor older people; I only wanted to bow to Jesus. Whether it was disrespectful or not, I didn't see why *in-saing* was important, especially at church.

"You need to bow and show respect to adults," my parents scolded me at home.

"Why is bowing important?"

"Korean culture. It's what you do when you see older people."

"But, we're in America. Why do you bring Korean culture to America, especially at church? There's hierarchy, and I don't like that."

"We go to a Korean church and we need to show respect to pastors, elders, and other adults. This is a sign of respect and honor."

"Respect? Honor? It's respectful when adults don't treat younger people as inferior or when *ahjummas* and *ahjusshis* don't talk behind other people's backs. Shouldn't we value others as much as ourselves? Why do the *janglos* think being an elder is a high position and desire a lot of respect? Shouldn't pastors and elders be more humble and caring instead of barking at –"

"Ssshhttt!" Dad cut me off. "You need to follow tradition and respect elders."

Rules, regulations, and traditions were embedded in the Korean immigrant church culture. Whether it was Confucianism, Korean culture, or Christian principles, figuring out which principle belonged to which culture and religion was confusing. Bowing and other "churchy" acts didn't really value or empower humans. For many adults, church was a place to show off and create a mirage of success in front of others: service, hard work, honor, and obedient children who were good-looking and smart. Parents pretended to be well and healthy at church, smiling, laughing, greeting elders and deacons, and serving food to pastors. For us children, despite what we didn't like, we were the byproduct of their behaviors. What we observed and learned trickled down to us.

As a female at a Presbyterian Korean immigrant church, I was limited in what I could do, despite my heart to serve others.

"I would like to serve at church," I asked the youth and college pastor.

"Well, since you are a female, you can help with the food ministry or children's ministry."

"Can I teach the boys?"

"No, you are a female. You can teach females or young children but not males your age. The Bible states women can't teach men."

Female teachers taught at schools and at universities, and there were female business leaders. It didn't make sense to me that male church members were okay when females taught non-church related materials outside of church, but it was not okay for females to teach inside church. I felt like I got the short end of the stick for being born female and attending a Presbyterian church that limited my service opportunities. But rather than becoming embittered, I served in the food ministry and took care of young children.

"Remember to treat and value others as yourselves," my high school and college pastors informed me at various times.

"What about homeless people?" I asked.

"Them, too."

"Then, how come you didn't help the homeless person down the street? Or what about the outcast student that was picked on by the more popular students?"

"Sarai, there's a time and place. Be quiet and listen to the sermon. You will become mature one day." I wondered if they were talking about my physical attributes or my intellectual capacity to understand humanity and our idiosyncrasies.

Throughout my younger years, I had a difficult time figuring out these apparent contradictions and needed to find what was true and false based on the Bible. The Bible stated to value people as themselves, but wherever I went, church, school, and society created dividing lines based on class, money, status, title, skin color, and more. Teachers, pastors, and other people talked about helping others, but they were reluctant to lend a hand during their off-duty hours. Rich people had difficulty seeing poor people through the eyes of Jesus. If they did, they would share their wealth with the poorer classes because, ultimately, we bought their products that increased their earning power. In addition, pastors, teachers, and other people jokingly made fun of each other, students used sarcastic remarks to others, yo-mama jokes and you so ugly jokes spread like wildfire, and the students who didn't fit the norm were neglected and bullied.

In my early twenties, many peers left the church when they were old enough to drive or go to college. The contradictions may have been a reason for a drop in church attendance, although those who left due to distaste in church religion also had their own set value-systems and created opinions based on their own ideologies of what was inappropriate or appropriate. We were all walking contradictions.

Despite the contradictions, I still had a longing to know the truth. For me, knowing if God really existed was important because I didn't want to worship a false God and pay dividends to the church's funds. I've always wondered if there was a way for Christians to be truly Christian without the fluff. I desired authenticity, if there were such a thing.

"I always went to church, but knowing the real God was difficult to grasp," a young twenty-something year old man said in front of the pulpit. He was sharing his testimony at a Korean American church, one of the churches I visited during my church-hopping days. "I'd always gone to church and did the church thing, but I didn't know if God was real."

"Go on," the pastor said on the side of the stage.

"For some of you, you've gone to church because your parents took you. It was a Korean tradition or immigrant experience. However, in our late teens and twenties, you began to fall away and question. You question your existence, your purpose in life, and if God is real."

I leaned forward and noticed others were, too. My life, while on the surface vibrant and full of exciting adventures, was mundane and empty at the end of the day. Whether I went dancing at Korean clubs, went to friends' parties, or hung out with friends, I felt a sense of emptiness and loneliness. Emotions rose and fell like a rollercoaster. I, too, wanted to know my purpose, why I was born, and if God were real.

"I closed my bedroom door. I was sick of life. I couldn't live my life like a broken record," the young man stated. I, too, couldn't live my life like he had.

"The Bible stated to draw near to God and He will draw near to you. It was now or never. Was God real? I told God I wasn't going to leave my room until He revealed himself. I read the Bible, prayed, and waited."

Could this be true? Could God reveal Himself in his bedroom? Warm liquid filled my bulging eyes.

"And there was a sound so great. 'I am He, I am the Lord!' God said." Tears streamed down his face and he began to hyperventilate.

"He became real and my heart and mind and body could not deny what I'd experienced and heard. God was real. It was then and there I gave my entire life to Jesus, and I am now going to

Japan for missions."

Warm liquid streamed down my face. Other people were also crying and shaking. After many years of attending church as routine, I heard from a peer, someone, a regular person, who shared with me that God was real. Aside from his testimony, a Korean man was crying on stage, and that to me was powerful.

While he shared his story, I, too, desired to hear God's voice. As I sat on the church pew; suddenly, an incident two years prior illuminated my mind. God had taken me back to the time when I had heard His voice warning me not to ride my royal blue motorcycle on Palomar Mountain.

On that particular Saturday morning during my senior year in college, I pressed the ignition switch on my motorcycle, and right above the handle, I saw a vision of my accident as if a movie were playing. Then, I heard a deep resounding voice, "Don't go today. You'll get into an accident." Deep in my spirit I knew the Voice was from God, but acting like a rebellious, blonde/orangey-haired Korean who liked the excitement of life, riding that morning was another opportunity to have fun. Ignoring both the vision and the Voice, I made my decision to ride, and I paid the consequences.

After the accident, my mother took me to see a healing pastor regarding my legs. The woman next to the pastor picked my coat as if she were throwing something away, but there was no lint or hair on it. I thought she was quite strange. The pastor, a tall, white, and thin-framed man, said I needed to repent and come back to God. He prayed for my legs and then sent me off. I perceived he was a charlatan, someone who prayed and wanted offering money. Though I questioned the pastor's healing prayers and the church's religious customs, I still attended Sunday service. Yet, going to church seemed like a task and not a place to have a real encounter with God. I questioned His existence.

In addition to my swollen legs that ached on a daily basis, I became a preschool teacher after college. Although I enjoyed educating the children, it was an anxiety-provoking experience that resulted in my having asthma, and besides my physical ailments, I was at a loss with my personal life. Eventually, the accident, the repetitive life that carried no meaningful purpose, and my bleak path were too much to handle. I was in spiritual, physical, emotional, and mental pain, and at my rate, I didn't want to continue living my current life. I needed help.

Towards the end of December of my 24th year, I did what the young Korean man had said in his testimony. If God revealed Himself to the man, why not me, I had thought. And so, I closed my bedroom door and waited until God revealed Himself to let me know if He was real. If He didn't, I would end my life.

God did not show up—Jesus in dazzling white clothing didn't walk into my room, nor stretch out his pierced hands so I could touch them and dispel my doubt like I had wanted.

After two weeks of waiting, crying, and desiring for a sign, I was ready to give up but still clung to a shred of hope. At that moment, a resounding voice unexpectedly echoed in my vacant room.

"Stop crying. Your sins are forgiven."

Awe-struck but still doubting if I had really heard God, I asked Him to get rid of my asthma as a sign of His existence.

"If I have faith as small as a mustard seed, I could move the mountain, and it will move. In the name of Jesus, I ask you to heal me of my asthma!" My request was not a plea but a strong statement, as if I could actually move a mountain.

The next day, I coughed my last phlegm, and the water that filled my legs disappeared. He was real.

What Was College About?

College was not mandatory; it was an option for many students, including Korean Americans. Many people assumed all second-generation Korean Americans attended universities, but this was not true. A handful of my Korean friends didn't go to college, and some of them who did, were not able to finish. Then, there was a subset, including myself, who actually went and finished college.

Going to college and finishing was a miracle. What I learned in high school did not fully prepare me to become successful for college, particularly in studying, reading, and taking exams. The fast-paced classes and long lectures required me to study daily and read multiple books and chapters in order to synthesize the complicated theories, names, and topics within a short period.

"I told you to study at your desk," Mom told me after I informed her that college was difficult. She thought studying at my desk with my back erect would help me retain information and do well in school. "You need better study habits," she scolded me.

"You don't understand. College in America is different. I just need a new brain!" I told her.

"*Aigoo.* You should have studied the right way when you were younger. You should have listened to me when I told you to be a good student."

"What is the right way?" I sincerely desired to finding a method to do well in college.

After taking psychology courses, I learned that underlining different sections in my book, then highlighting them, would help me retain more information. After coloring my entire book with different highlighters and underlining important words in preparation for my exams, rather than remembering the information, I only remembered what particular color I had highlighted a certain page.

College was difficult despite the fact that I looked smart. I failed my science course and barely received passing grades during my first and second year. I did study; but then again, I ate, listened to music, and hung out with friends. There was too much to do in college. In high school, I had to take five to six mandatory classes on a daily basis. In college, taking three courses once a week was considered a full load. To top it off, it wasn't mandatory to attend my classes. I went to a large public university and with 500 plus students, the professor didn't know or maybe didn't care if I was present. Freedom reigned in college.

Without a strong foundation of who I was and what I was supposed to do, this freedom led to a lot of wandering. To my dismay, going off task became a major issue, and I had to organize my life on a weekly basis, because if I didn't, hanging out with my friends and cultivating new friendships preoccupied my study time. As a bubbly, social butterfly, scheduling my study time was imperative because I came to realize that I didn't have the mental capacity to grasp information faster than my classmates. Poisoned with the concept that Asians were innately intelligent compared to white, blacks, and Latinos, thoughts of stupidity and learning issues flared when my multi-ethnic friends received A's and B's, and I received a C, and a D in my general psychology courses. It was embarrassing. I couldn't tell people I was struggling, especially not my parents.

Despite taking courses to fulfill my major requirements that would help me secure a future career, college was mostly about learning how to become an adult, especially when it came to strengthening my communication and life skills with roommates, suitemates, and friends.

I had to live in a rectangular dorm room with a roommate I had never met in my life. The university did some kind of matchmaking because my roommate was also a second generation Korean American who grew up in Los Angeles County. We learned how to acclimate to the new college culture and to each other. We were Koreans, but we were very different. She came from a different part of Los Angeles County, and from my experience with her, I came to the realization that depending on where Koreans lived and how they were brought up, they were a unique bunch. College broadened my understanding that every person had unique differences, and that their lives and how they were socialized influenced the way they thought, behaved, and treated people.

As for myself, I originally had the hope of starting fresh when I went to college by establishing new friendships and freeing myself from my family struggles and altering parts of the Korean cultural traditions that I disliked. However, both my positive and negative experiences, along with my *ka-shis*, were appendages that stuck with me.

Even though I perceived myself to be a functional person without having had traumatic events that prevented me from living a quality life, the handful of psychology, sociology, and human development courses I took revealed I had problems. I had accumulated a memory bank of positive and negative experiences, and sometimes, deeply wounded pain.

My direct experiences observing and interacting with Suzi, Jenny, Ken, Young, Johnny, Little d, Sarah, Gi Shin, and other people affected me as a young adult. Their influence became evident when I met new people who resembled them, or when I found patterns with people's personalities and behaviors because of where they came from, what choices they made in life, and more.

"Hi, my name is Sarai. And you?"

"Gi Shin."

"Nice to meet you. Interesting name. I once knew a Gi Shin during my high school years."

My heart fluttered and flashbacks of the old Gi Shin ignited; and despite telling myself that the new Gi Shin was different from the old Gi Shin, my mind, heart, and soul would not comply with my requests. The feelings and thoughts I had of old Gi Shin projected onto the new Gi Shin. The *ka-shis* poked out of my body at inopportune moments. Either I avoided her or was mean to her. Sometimes, I snapped at her, and, on rare moments, I completely lashed out at her.

Then, there were times when I met up with Johnnie, the Korean American raver who took ecstasy, or a guy named D. Seeing them reminded me of Little d, and led me to wonder how he was doing. Though it had been many years since I had last seen him, I couldn't help but hope the best for his future.

From my constant observations of people's lives, I discovered that my college friends, friends or acquaintances back home, people throughout society, and I had *ka-shi* that intentionally or unintentionally projected onto others. Our past wounds, those undesired rotten *ka-shis,* resided in our souls and pierced out of our bodies.

When we complained or talked negatively about our past and current circumstances and unresolved issues, or when we were frustrated, angry, bitter, jealous, irritated, anxious, stressed, and depressed, *ka-shis* were stuck inside our souls. Knowing people had *ka-shis* was evident, and many people either searched for answers or tried to bury their *ka-shis.*

We needed answers, but, to my disappointment, my college academic courses did not offer much help. I had to find other ways to uncover past wounds and pluck out *ka-shi.*

Taking Out Our *Ka-Shis*

"Welcome to MAPS. My name is Sarai, and my purpose in life is to help you discover your destiny and map out your path so you can live quality lives." High school students, college students, and adults sat in a crowded room at the program office.

"How many of you have dreams?" Hands shot up all over the room.

"We all have dreams, but let me be frank with you. Not many people will fulfill their ultimate dream destiny." The faces that had smiles turned to frowns.

Throughout my daily experiences with people, I observed, heard, and examined why many of us were not living to our full potential, despite our desired to live quality lives. There were too many obstacles impeding our paths and the solutions to our unanswered questions. The choices we made resulted in different outcomes that left us in pain. One mistake consequently led Jim to lose his college scholarship. One decision to purge prevented Jenny from eating *galbi* for the rest of her life. One family who wanted to look perfect on the outside led Suzi to hide her *ka-shi* and live with pain. One hope to excel in school and attend prestigious colleges led some of my peers to compromise their physical, emotional, and mental health. For many people who were not able to overcome such issues, how would they reach their destinies when another obstacle came their way?

"How many of you have obstacles?"

The people in the room raised their hands.

"We all have issues," I stated plainly. "Some of us keep them and try to suppress them. Others try to discard them only to realize those issues come back in subtle to adverse ways. Then, there are those few who have been able to successfully overcome obstacles without holding onto any bitterness, anger, and jealousy. Would you like to live a fulfilled life and move forward without obstacles impeding your way?"

Heads nodded.

"Do you want to know the skills to overcome obstacles that come in your daily lives and who is patient with others, forgiving of others, and not someone who is easily temperamental, frustrated, angry, and irritable?"

The group's eyes glistened and hands reached out towards me as if yearning for answers they could not find.

"Although the actual program usually lasts a year or more, I'm going to provide you with a portion of the program for the next 15 weeks. I will facilitate the process using questions, visualizations, lectures, and observations."

I paused and then asked one final time, "How many people want to live a quality life, discover their destinies and fulfill it, and overcome obstacles that come on a daily basis?"

All 30 hands were raised.

"The training I am about to share with you will take you down a painful road, but I promise, if you stay with me, by the time this training is over, you will learn what *ka-shis* have been holding you down and have the opportunity to take many *ka-shis* out of your system. You will be transformed. Again, this program is supposed to be longer, but I'm going to provide you with a shortened, condensed version. Just to be clear. I am not going to jam information down your throat or hurt you, although there will be many occasions you will feel pain in your heart. What I am about to do is to help you open your eyes, reflect, and observe your life, the lives of others, and society. You choose how you want to continue living your life. I'll provide you with the "how-tos," skills, and strategies to overcome any obstacle that impedes your way. The only thing I ask you is to not drop out. If you happen to do so, you may carry unwanted *ka-shis* with you into your present and future circumstances. I'm here to help you finish only if you allow me to."

"Everyone," I proclaimed, "we are very strong. We don't need to show how strong we are by showing off, being prideful or putting other people down, because those who do are actually weak. The strong person is the person who goes last, who lifts others forward rather than trying to climb on top of people, and who gives rather than receives."

"Whenever you see people being bullied, remember that the bullies were once bullied. Their parents, friends, and others may have hurt them in some way. Or maybe they were bystanders. We can't remember everything that has happened to us, but the effects are evident. Bullies don't know how to heal from their past and the wounds are pierced deep inside their souls. Many people who are hurt on the inside cover up their issues with a proud heart and arrogant personality. They have no qualms about putting other people down, saying critical and bitter words, and having a negative attitude. Whether they display these at all times or subtly, you can tell if people have *ka-shi*."

Their eyes widened.

"And whenever you see someone talking negatively or criticizing others in front of them or behind their backs, just remember, these people are insecure and unaware of what is most important in their lives. They are busy finding what is wrong with everyone else rather than finding out what they are supposed to do with their own lives and taking their *ka-shis* out. People who are secure and confident do not have to put others down. You can always find fake people by listening to what they have to say about others."

"You all have been bullied and have bullied others. We are one and the same. No matter where we go, we will always be affected by what we see, hear, taste, smell, and touch in both positive and negative ways that can help us or destruct our very lives--and each other."

"Society, media, schools, and places we've lived, *ka-shis* are everywhere. People's *ka-shis* mix with other people's *ka-shis*. These *ka-shis* began when babies were in their mothers' wombs. A mother's thoughts and feelings that were affected by society and her upbringing affect the psyche of her baby. By the time the babies come out of their mothers' wombs, they have *ka-shis*, too."

Their mouths opened like fish seeking food. They leaned forward, yearning to find the answers to their social, family, and relational problems. I had inherited a golden key to unlock my soul and heal from my wounds. However, this gold looked rather like a hard, buttery rock, and it took a lot of refining and training to make it into a lustrous golden color. I was about to use my golden key to start the lessons.

"Some people have strived to live quality lives. Some people never searched for them or gave up. What I am about to share with you will unlock the keys to your heart, mind, and soul. I remember the journey of discovering the path to pull out my *ka-shi*. It took nearly twenty years to search for answers, and I've been in training for 10 years, and went to college for 15 years, in order to be your tour guide to show you that the impossible, arduous journey can be possible."

"Some of you during this three month program will learn why you do and say certain things in life, and how to overcome pain and hurt so you can live quality lives. You will get the condensed version to help you turn your life around. Are you ready?" Their heads nodded.

"We will do a lot of soul searching, but in the end, you will come out of this program free, light, and full of life. This program is called Project SPICES. Let's spice up your life."

I stared at them and they peered back, wondering if I were telling the truth.

Throughout the following 15 weeks, I shared with the class my positive memories and colorful stories, filled with people who cared, supported, and loved me, especially the One who saved my life from misery and death. They, in turn, shared with me their stories and allowed their hidden pain to come out.

One of them, Stephanie, had attempted suicide, was bullied, and suffered from depression. Recalling the fear that I had experienced with Gi Shin, I could identify with Stephanie's pain and didn't want her to go through the same cycle of terror and self-hatred. After the program, she no longer had a desire to kill herself, stopped having depression, and became a passionate leader. Eventually, Stephanie she reached out to the bully, who became her close friend.

Then, there was Dylan who once shared with a group of students and me that he wanted to buy a gun and shoot his bullies and the people he disliked. He reminded me of the student from the Columbine High School massacre. After the program, he had no desire to kill his classmates but to help them. He created school clubs, took on leadership roles, and now spends time socializing with people.

We began the 15 weeks with a big school of fish, but by the time the training was over, there were only 12 left. But they were 12 healthy fish who learned how to let go of their past wounds, forgive people who had hurt them, and accept and love others as themselves. Their lives were changed, but to what extent, I didn't know until they shared with me how their lives were changed.

A year later, one beautiful college student, Madelyn, expressed her deep gratitude for the program, saying, "I have learned that we have to forgive people around us in order to accept who we are and to forgive ourselves. It is important to love yourself for who you truly are, to learn how to cope with your feelings and to realize that what you believe of yourself is what is reflected unto others. So, love and forgive the people around you."

Madelyn's internal transform and external approach to expressing her feelings and living life with less *ka-shi* brought overwhelming tears of joy when I thought of her. Though the knowledge and skills were provided to her, she made the conscious choice to let go of anger and bitterness. Her hardened heart melted and she began healing from the sore wounds of multiple *ka-shis* that had once punctured her soul.

Two years later, Ruth, a current college student, expressed how I had taught her to live a quality life. Whether she truly learned what was taught would be determined by the way she lives her life during and after college. What we learn can only be determined by how we apply our understandings that leads us on a path to live quality lives or another path that does not.

For me, I've walked on a particular path, engaged in rich encounters with diverse people in various settings, and experienced what I had to go through to understand that my life was not about me, but about helping others. The *pojagi, bimbimbap,* and *jeon,* and the diverse people that came across my existence were learning opportunities to help me unpack how my *ka-shis* pierced my soul and affected me. Armed with this knowledge, I now share it so that others can heal, too.

Glossary

Note: Some of the Korean words are not in correct honorific or non-honorific form. Also, some of the words may not be "Korean"; Sarai created her own Korean words.

ahjumma – "aunt" but mainly used to call a married woman or older lady

ahjusshi – a man older than you

aigoo – "oh my god"

aju massiseo – it's very delicious

aleumdaun – beautiful, good-looking

appa – daddy

babo – stupid

banchan(s) – side dishes served with the main dish

banmal – informal, non-honorific Korean language when speaking to people younger than you or friends

bap da meoggo – finish your food

bibimbap – mixed rice

buchimgae – Korean pancake. See *jeon*

bulgogi – grilled marinated beef

byeoseul – lord and sir

chajangmyun – noodles with black bean sauce

daengjjang – soybean

daengjjang chigae – soybean paste soup made with fermented soybeans as a soup base with squash, onions, mushrooms, and tofu.

dolsot – hot stone bowl

dongchimi – watery radish

dosilak – lunch box

eomeoni – mother in honorific form

umma – mom

galbi – Korean BBQ beef

geugeo meoya – "what's that mean" in banmal (poor grammar)

gi shin – ghost

gochu – chili pepper

gochujang – chili pepper paste

gongbu – study

haembeogeo – hamburger

hajima – "stop" in non-honorific form

hakwon(s) – academy or cram school

halmoni – grandmother from father's side

hanguk mal heh – speak in Korean

hanyak – Korean oriental medicine

in-sa heh – to bow, a respectful approach to greet people in Korean customs

jeil-mas-iss-da – it is the best

jalang – boast

jang-jorim – brisket beef simmered in a sweet, dark brown
marinade made out of soy sauce

janglos – male church elders

jansoli – complain, undesirable talking when people are tired of hearing you speak

jeon – Korean pancake made with vegetables and

sometimes with seafood

jondaemal – honorific form used to speak to people older than you

jorim – dishes simmered in sauce

jorim banchans – side dishes that have been simmered in sauce

juh-guh moh ya – "what is that?", this phrase is poorly written in the Korean language.

ka-shi – fish bone

kkakdugi – radish kimchi

kimchi – variety of fermented vegetables

Konglish – Korean and English language

kyung – Lord and sir (kyung has different meanings depending on the Chinese character)

maeuntang – spicy seafood soup

massiso – good, delicious

meh-meh – a phrase used by adults when they tell their children they will get hit

mian hae . . .yo – I am sorry

moh – what

moh yeh gi heh suh – "What did they say?" (this phrase is poorly written in the Korean language

myulchi bokkeum – little fishies/anchovies

nabak-kimchi – kimchi made with cabbage

nae baega ap-poh – my stomach hurts (poorly written in the Korean language)

nah-moo – wood

namul banchans – seasoned vegetable dishes

namul muchim – seasoned bean sprouts

napo (nappeun) – colloquial word used to convey a bad person. (*Napo* was used to illustrate how Korean men were like napa kimchi—traditional, fermented, and common.)

neh – yes

noonchi – discernment

noraebang – karaoke, place where people sing in a private room

oh mae mae – "oh my my"

oi-sobagi – stuffed cucumber kimchi

ojingeochae bokkeum – sitr-fried dried squid

paebaes – physical and verbal beatings

pojagi – traditional Korean wrapping cloth

pyechajang – junkyard

sangchu – lettuce

sigeumchi namul – seasoned spinach salad

ttogbalo – straighten, do it right

ttong baes – belly fat or belly rolls

umma – mommy

unni – older sister, people call female servers out of politeness

weh – why

weh-halmoni – grandmother from mother's side

yang-bo – give in

yook gae jang – spicy beef soup made with leek, green bean sprouts, and other ingredients

Information that has been modified

Sister's name
Brother's name
People's names
Some of the characters in the vignettes were a combination of two people in order to protect their identities.

Gi Shin - two bullies combined as one person.

The End.

Thank you for reading!
For more information, please go to
www.maps4college.org and www.projectspices.com.

18703632R00103

Made in the USA
San Bernardino, CA
25 January 2015